# PRAISE FOR

"Since wisdom is found in a multitude of counselors it follows that in Proverbs we also have a multitude of counsel for many facets of our life. Terry Allen has pulled together a great selection of studies that will lead one down the path of wisdom. Take that path and read this book."

**Dr. Mark Bailey**
President, Dallas Theological Seminary

"*Wisdom: Life Lessons from the World's Wisest (and Richest) Man* is the answer to a culture struggling to determine right from wrong, and truth from falsehood. Terry Allen has taken the classic book of Proverbs and put its admonitions in a unique and user friendly format. His abundant illustrations of how wisdom works in real life help make this superb book a must read for students of all ages and stages of life."

**Michael Little**
Chairman, National Religious Broadcasters

"As a master chef combines ingredients, Terry Allen assembled the many bite-size nuggets of Solomon's wisdom into a five-course gourmet meal called, *Wisdom: Life Lessons from the World's Wisest (and Richest) Man*. What a fresh and appetizing presentation of God's wisdom in Proverbs."

**Jerry Dirmann**
Founder and Senior Pastor, The Rock
Anaheim, California

"Terry Allen has done a masterful work of bringing the wisdom of King Solomon's Proverbs into 21st century daily living. Insightful. Practical. Godly."

**Don Finto**
Pastor Emeritus
Belmont Church, Nashville, Tennessee
President/Founder, Caleb Company

"Wisdom—most of us desire more of it and many of us don't know where or how to get it. For years, I've encouraged leaders to turn to the Book of Proverbs for valuable teachings on the concept of wisdom for all areas of their lives, and now with the release of *Wisdom* by Terry Allen, I'll be adding this book to my recommended reading list. As the perfect partner to Proverbs, *Wisdom* explains the themes presented in Proverbs, and more importantly, breaks them down into simple, easily digestible terms. Whether you're a leader in business, at home or in your social circles—or simply desire to be one, *Wisdom* should be at the top of your reading list. Let this inspiring and relevant book be your guide to better understand the teaching of Proverbs—and you'll be well on your way to discovering wisdom in all aspects of your own life."

**Greg Provenzano**
President and Co-Founder ACN INC.

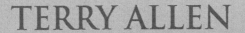

# TERRY ALLEN

# WISDOM

## LIFE LESSONS FROM THE WORLD'S
## WISEST (AND RICHEST) MAN

FOREWORD BY
## DR. TOM COBURN, U.S. SENATE (RET.)

Wisdom: Life Lessons from the World's Wisest (and Richest) Man
Copyright © 2018, 2020 Terry Allen. All rights reserved.

All Scripture citations are from the English Standard Version (ESV) unless otherwise indicated.

Lampion House Publishing, LLC
P.O. Box 932
Silverton, OR 97381

ISBN: SBN 978-1-7345067-2-3
Library of Congress Control Number

Formatting by J.R. Miller and cover design by Amy Cole, JPL Design Solutions

Printed in the United States of America

TERRY ALLEN

# WISDOM

LIFE LESSONS FROM THE WORLD'S
WISEST (AND RICHEST) MAN

LAMPION
HOUSE
Publishing

# DEDICATION

This book is dedicated to my father and mother,
Bill and Glenda Allen
whose lives have served as true models of wisdom.

I also want to dedicate it to the people throughout my life who invested their time to show me the value of living according to the instructions found in the book of Proverbs; Donnie and Edwina Pruett, Faye Smith, the late Tom Miller, Mike Galiga, Bill Gaultiere, Steve Harper, Ed Buckham, Jeff Ling, and Ron Holt.

# ACKNOWLEDGMENTS

I want to thank H. Wayne House, my editor, without whose tireless work this book could not have been realized. Thank you to Tim Demy and Amy Cole at JPL for your help and patience in formatting and layout. I also want to thank Bill Wichterman, whose proofreading, feedback, his encouragement on this project, and his friendship and example of statesmanship over the last 30 years have been more valuable than he knows. Thanks to Jon Jones for taking the time to read through the manuscript and for the encouragement! I also want to thank my best friend—my lovely wife Laurie. Thank you for being there, for listening, for the advice and the encouragement.

# TABLE OF CONTENTS

# FOREWORD

Words come easily to most of us, but it is actions that matter—what we actually do that makes all the difference. As a physician who practiced for over 25 years, I have seen the consequences of poor decision making among families. Self-inflicted wounds—poor decisions that have impacted the health, the quality of relationships, the quality of life and even the life spans of many patients. Some of these decisions have resulted in the worst heartaches, alienation and long running feuds that one can imagine. The sad truth is that many of these mistakes and their consequences could have been prevented through better, wiser choices, by applying wisdom to one's daily decisions.

As a Member of Congress, and then as a U.S. Senator, I have seen how unwise decisions—scaled up and applied to our culture at large, have brought devastating consequences for our nation, impacting lives on a scale that is nearly incalculable.

We all need wisdom. Our culture needs wisdom. Our nation—now more than ever—needs wisdom.

This book is about Wisdom. It is about making wise choices and exploring the ancient scriptures, which are extremely practical in their application to us today. The lessons in this book apply to all of us— from the wealthiest, to the poorest, from the experienced senior to the young adult, from the celebrity to the obscure. I want my children and grandchildren to read this book and learn from it because it is a wonderful guide for living.

I have known Terry Allen for over 25 years. He is the right person to write this book—not just because he has studied the book of Proverbs for over 40 years, but because he lives out what he teaches. I have seen him model and mentor others in the key teachings contained herein. I highly commend this book to you. It has much to teach us.

Tom Coburn, M.D.
U.S. Senate (OK-ret.)
August 2017

# INTRODUCTION

Life is hard. It seems that regardless of how good things might work out on occasion, the challenges of life just keep coming at you, don't they? Each and every new day brings new struggles and new difficulties. And they keep coming. They don't let up. They just keep coming—at what sometimes feels like an unbearable pace. Bills to pay, issues with our kids, health problems, marriage issues to resolve, the stresses of work. You know the challenges—rough seas to navigate even when everything is going well—even when we make all the right decisions. But life's challenges get much, much harder when we make bad decisions. Bad decisions are painful. And they usually cost a lot of money and often alter the course of our lives.

> Foolish decisions make life profoundly more difficult and complicated than it needs to be.

I see people every day—and I'm sure you see them too—people who, in spite of their best attempts to navigate life's difficult waters, make very bad decisions. Poor, unwise and foolish decisions. And in doing so, they needlessly complicate their lives, cost themselves money and cause themselves and those they love pain. These foolish decisions make life profoundly more difficult and complicated than it needs to be.

Unwise decisions. I see them over and over in the lives of others. I see them in my own life. If you are honest, you see them in yours, too.

It's evident that we as a society—and all of us as individuals—need wisdom. Real wisdom. Not trite snippets or catchy sound bites. Not quick fixes from the chattering class on cable news shows. Not self-help from this week's hottest conference speaker. Not talk show blather. We need true wisdom. The kind that helps us make really good, quality decisions that can spare us pain and heartache. Money-saving, life-improving decisions.

We don't seem to hear much about wisdom in our society today. And unless you consciously try to seek them out, you run into very few, truly wise people these days. Wisdom is not a common trait found among the masses. This is because wisdom is not easy to come by. It is not easy to acquire. It takes both effort and diligence. In order to acquire wisdom, one must be intentional about it.

> In order to acquire wisdom, one must be intentional about it.

But there is a man in history who had much to say on the subject, and if you are willing to listen, he left a treasure that still speaks powerfully to you and me today. He is a man of the ages who offered advice and help for our lives. He was not perfect, and he did make mistakes, but his wisdom was profound and widely recognized. In fact, he was known in history as the wisest man who had ever lived. He was King Solomon of ancient Israel. He was a fascinating man who had much to say, and if you'll consider what he had to say, it could change your life.

Change your life? Really? That's a grandiose claim. We hear that phrase thrown around a lot, but nevertheless, it is true. What Solomon left us could change your life. Intrigued? Then keep reading.

So who was King Solomon and what made him so wise? He was the second son of King David and his wife Bathsheba— yes that Bathsheba—the "other woman" and the central figure involved in King David's greatest moral failure and most embarrassing political scandal. When his father David was aging, Solomon ascended the throne of ancient Israel. The year was roughly 950 B.C.

Israel's King Solomon is described in the Bible by his two most notable traits: his wisdom and his wealth. In fact, he was far richer than all the kings of the ancient world—literally the richest man of his day. Even by today's standards, where barons and billionaires circle the globe in private jets and custom yachts, Solomon's wealth was impressive.

The revenue from trading that flowed through his hands over the span of his reign has been estimated at between $40 billion and one trillion.[1] This figure doesn't include what he received in domestic taxes, or what he received from his father David as an inheritance. In practical terms, he had more than he knew what to do with, evidenced by the fact that all of King Solomon's personal household items such as goblets and table settings were pure gold. Silver, in fact was so plentiful in Jerusalem during his reign as to be considered of little value. King Solomon was wealthier than all the other kings of other nations before him. And none of Israel's kings after him were his equal—financially, or politically.

Besides amassing a fortune for both himself and his nation, he has been credited with creating a standard of living that was the envy of surrounding nations. He used gold as an economic tool to unify Israel into one of the strongest nations on earth and an economic powerhouse of the ancient world. He built a fleet of trading ships—a rare accomplishment in ancient times that brought gold, silver, ivory, exotic horses, apes and even baboons to Israel. In construction, architecture, and even in transportation, he charted a unique path. Rather than conquering nearby nations and taking their raw materials by force, he fashioned trade agreements, thereby tapping the intellect and skill from artisans and advice from the advisors of other nations. The good-will he enjoyed from neighboring nations gained him unequaled credibility and favor among the kings of the known world.

In Jerusalem, he built the magnificent temple to Yahweh, the God of the Hebrews. This temple was the global architectural wonder of the day. He overlaid much of it with pure gold. The legends and tales of King Solomon's mines that yielded this gold are renowned to this day.

He investigated the arts and sciences, specifically botany and agriculture. He became a leading expert on philosophy, literature and poetry. He composed thousands of proverbs and hundreds of poems and songs. He wrote three books of the Bible: the Song of Solomon, Proverbs and Ecclesiastes. Like the pharaohs of Egypt before him, Nebuchadnezzar of ancient Babylon, Alexander the Great of ancient Greece and Rome's Julius Caesar, who ruled centuries after him, Solomon was recognized as *the* great world leader of his day. But unlike these other world leaders, his great-est achievement was not in his military conquests, but in how he was able to harness the peace and prosperity of his nation into improvements for the lives of his people. Unlike many other kings, he did not obtain his kingdom through conquering neigh-boring states. His father David had fought and won those battles in the previous generation. But Solomon built impressively upon the accomplishments of his father David by leading Israel to a cultural height that was unimagined by anyone up to that time. He was a man of ferocious appetite for variety, for learning and for life. The Old Testament book of 2 Chronicles describes him this way,

> Thus King Solomon excelled all the kings of the earth in riches and in wisdom. And all the kings of the earth sought the presence of Solomon to hear his wisdom, which God had put into his mind. Every one of them brought his present, articles of silver and of gold, gar-

ments, myrrh, spices, horses, and mules, so much year by year. (2 Chron. 9:22-25)

The book of 1 Kings also describes a visit from a neighboring queen from what is believed to be modern day Yemen. She is referred to as the Queen of Sheba. And she was so intrigued by Solomon's reputation that she brought a visiting delegation to Jerusalem just to see if what she had heard was indeed true. She also came to test him with difficult questions. According to 1 Kings, Solomon answered every one of her questions; nothing was too hard for him to explain to her. When she saw the palace Solomon had built, the food on his table, the seating of his officials, the attending servants and the magnificent temple that he had built for worship, she was overwhelmed. She said to him:

The report was true that I heard in my own land of your words and of your wisdom, but I did not believe the reports until I came and my own eyes had seen it. And behold, the half was not told me. Your wisdom and prosperity surpass the report that I heard. Happy are your men! Happy are your servants, who continually stand before you and hear your wisdom! (1 Kings 10:6–8)

The Queen of Sheba found that Solomon's wisdom and wealth actually *exceeded his reputation.* As a parting gift, she gave the king gold, large quantities of spices, and precious stones. She went back to her native land in awe. Truly no one had seen anything like him. During Solomon's reign, leaders from all over the world sought audience with him. He was described in Scripture as the wisest man in the world, and the queen's visit certainly seems to confirm this.

King Solomon is unique among world leaders for one other reason. Unlike Egypt's pharaohs or Alexander the Great or Julius Caesar, we have an abundance of Solomon's writings. These works leave an impressive volume of writings that are not only penned from his hand, but writings that God Himself is considered to have inspired.

The most important of these works is the book of Proverbs. To many, this collection of proverbs is often passed over as quaint little niceties, or little "nuggets" of truth or just good sayings from a wise man. But they are, in reality, much, much more. They offer practical help for daily living. They offer directions for success. They offer profound advice on personal growth and life management skills. And they are as timely today as when they were written. They are, in fact, timeless lessons for life. The book of Proverbs is comprised of thirty-one chapters that have been with us for centuries, but relative to the rest of Scripture, they have rarely been systematically examined and applied to modern living.

How do they apply to today's modern culture? Did King Solomon have anything to say about modern issues? Does King Solomon's advice stand the test of time?

This book synthesizes the book of Proverbs into a digestible and usable tool for modern culture. It is a result of a lifetime of study of this ancient treasure. It outlines twenty-seven major themes and topics that are repeated in various passages throughout Proverbs. These passages provide real world answers—not just pleasant sound bites, or helpful phrases for refrigerator magnets, but workable, real life strategies to handle some of our most pressing concerns on the fundamental issues you and I deal with everyday: money and business, relationships, sex and family issues, leadership, personal development and spirituality.

This book dissects the entire book of Proverbs and applies it to everyday modern life. It offers sound advice upon which to build a successful life. I believe you will discover a true treasure in these pages—a treasure that will pay huge dividends in your life, in your future, and in the future of those you love.

PART I

# THE NATURE
# OF WISDOM

# 1

# WISDOM IS AVAILABLE TO EVERYONE

O kay, you are ready to glean from the wisest man in the world, to sit at the feet of the wisest sage that has ever put pen to paper. If you are expecting to find principles for successful living, then you are looking in the right place. If you are among the 225 million people in the U.S. that hold the Bible as divinely inspired[2] you might consider this book an ultimate self-help book. But before we get to the fun part that tells you how to enjoy the many benefits that accompany wisdom, we have to place this issue in its proper context. And therefore, we must confront false assumptions up front. This book is about getting to the truth. It is about dealing with reality. Not with the world as we would like it to be, but with the world as it is. And one of the misconceptions that many people live under is that life is supposed to be "fair." But the truth is that life is not fair.

Let me say it again. Life is not fair. It's really not (at least in the way you probably define fairness). If you have been living under the misconception that life is supposed to be fair you are probably a very frustrated person because chances are, you are not getting what you deserve, are you? You haven't received your

11

"fair" share in life, right? I mean, you don't have to look very far to see that other people all around you have more, do more, make more, and seem to enjoy it more than you do, right? If you are honest with yourself, you'll agree that life often seems this way. Often it *is* this way.

No, life is not fair. We are not all given the same opportunities in life. Some people are born into great privilege and some into severe poverty. Some have every opportunity handed to them on a silver platter, while some people just can't seem to catch a break. Some are gifted with interpersonal skills and seem to have an amazing capacity for making money, making friends or finding their true love. For others, those aspirations seem next to impossible. No, life is not fair. We don't all have the same opportunities in life. We don't all have the same chances for success.

Some people don't handle this reality very well. Many become quite bitter about it because they don't have what they think they deserve. If you haven't ever stopped to seriously consider it before, I would strongly suggest that you consider this and process this thought: Life is not fair. There will always be those around you that are better off than you, regardless of how successful you are (or think you are). Likewise, regardless of how tough things are, things could always get worse. No matter how bad things get, there will always be someone else worse off than you. So many circumstances are just beyond your control.

Well then, if life is not fair, are you saying, Terry, that God is not fair? No, that is not what I'm saying. God is, I believe (and as you will see in the pages of this book) fair and just. However, to many people, it may appear that God is not fair. But remember, you and I have a limited view of life. We can only see our life and our circumstances up to this point. We can't see into the future. Nor can we see life from the perspective of other people—or from God's eternal perspective. And with our extremely limited view, it will undoubtedly appear at times that life is not "fair."

You must bring yourself to the realization that your opportunities in life are going to be unique to you. You will have more opportunities, skills, talents and money than some people; and you will have less opportunities, skills, talents and money than others. These are some of the many circumstances that are just beyond your control.

But, there are some things that you can control. And that's where this book begins. This book can help you focus on those things that are within your control. Someone once said (and I agree with this whole-heartedly and repeat it to others often), "The issue is not so much what is happening to you; the issue is how you respond to what is happening to you." This may sound callous, but think about it for a minute. In your life, no matter where you are, you may not be able to control what is happening to you at the moment, but how you respond to your circumstances is very, very much in your control.

> The issue is not so much what is happening to you; the issue is how you respond to what is happening to you.

Each day you are faced with decisions that will determine your future. And regardless of the opportunities or lack of opportunities that you have been given, regardless of the ways that others have hurt you, regardless of how unfair life has been to you—no one else is responsible for you. You are responsible for you. When all is said and done, you will bear the consequences of your decisions.

Each day of your life presents you with decisions that you must make on how you respond to the unkind acts of others and to the harsh words spoken to you, decisions on how you treat people, hundreds of daily decisions that in total, determine your character,

> When all is said and done, you will bear the consequences of your decisions.

that determine who you are. And these daily decisions—the words that you say, the tone of voice you use, your actions and lack of actions—are in reality the great equalizer. Because no matter who you are, whether you are rich or poor, feeble or healthy, young or old, mistreated or privileged, you, I, and every person on the planet, have the opportunity to start over.

Each day offers the opportunity to change direction and do something different. Each day, regardless of the circumstances in which you find yourself, you are given the opportunity to begin again, to get another chance to line up at the starting line. Each day is your opportunity to do something, to make decisions that no one else can make. Every day you are faced with opportunities. What will you do with them? Okay, so you're not as well off as your neighbor, but you are not as bad off as others you know. But regardless of your conditions, you can begin at the starting line with every other person. You can respond in wisdom or with foolishness, with kindness or malice, in confidence or in fear.

And how you respond will determine your future from this day forward.

Your life doesn't have to be, and probably will not be, like it has always been. You see, change is one of the only certainties that this life offers. And what kind of changes come to your life are determined in large part by you and by the hundreds of decisions you will make starting *today*. So regardless of where you are or what you have done, how you've been hurt, or how you've hurt others, you can hit the reset button.

> Your life doesn't have to be, and probably will not be, like it has always been.

You can start again today by making wise decisions. Or, you can make foolish decisions. It's up to you. Wisdom is available for the taking. Wisdom is available for you.

In three distinct passages, the book of Proverbs metaphorically describes wisdom as a woman who is shouting to all mankind... to you... each and every day. She is seen as a wealthy and gracious host inviting you to enjoy her hospitality in Proverbs 9:1-6:

> Wisdom has built her house;
> she has hewn her seven pillars.
>
> She has slaughtered her beasts; she has mixed her wine;
> she has also set her table.
>
> She has sent out her young women to call
> from the highest places in the town,
>
> "Whoever is simple, let him turn in here!"
> To him who lacks sense she says,
>
> "Come, eat of my bread and drink of the wine I have
> mixed.
> Leave your simple ways, and live, and walk in the way
> of insight."

And again, in Proverbs 1:20-23:

> Wisdom cries aloud in the street,
> in the markets she raises her voice;
>
> at the head of the noisy streets she cries out;
> at the entrance of the city gates she speaks:
>
> "How long, O simple ones, will you love being simple?
> How long will scoffers delight in their scoffing and fools
> hate knowledge?
>
> If you turn at my reproof, behold, I will pour out my spirit
> to you;
> I will make my words known to you.

In both of these passages (and again in Prov. 8:1-11) wisdom is compared to a gracious host that is inviting each of us to an extravagant feast. Wisdom is encouraging her guests, "Come here, eat my food ... come, let me share with you my benefits." It is an equal opportunity invitation. It is the ultimate equal opportunity invitation.

Wisdom is like rain as it's falling from the skies. It's all around us. Obtaining it doesn't require special status. It is available for everyone that will make a conscious decision to look up and receive. There are no special abilities required. Everyone can take advantage of her offer.

Many people see themselves as victims—frequently comparing themselves to someone else that has more opportunity, more money, more of this or more of that. Many people believe that they never get a break. But the truth is that there are opportunities every single day for you to make wise decisions and to make poor decisions. All around you are examples of people that have decided to start making wise decisions—and their lives have been dramatically changed because of it. There are people all around you that have refused to let their circumstances dictate their future, people who chose to take wisdom up on her offer and decided to make better decisions than they did the day before.

People such as Nate Larkin of Nashville, Tennessee, who like millions of men in our nation, became addicted to pornography. Enduring his humiliating moral struggle for five years, he was unable to pull himself out of his private world of addiction until he was caught and confronted by his wife. Her confrontation forced Nate to either get help or lose everything he had worked for. Fortunately, Nate made a wise choice and got the help he needed. It took time and a significant commitment to work through the issues that lead to his addiction, but his marriage was saved and today he helps counsel other men through their porn addiction.[3]

Sometimes choosing wisdom doesn't involve leaving a destructive lifestyle. It can involve a simple decision to change the way one has always viewed themselves—or others. Or to no longer tolerate those things they've always tolerated. We all know of Rosa Parks, the Alabama seamstress who refused to suffer the continued abuse of discrimination inflicted on her because of her race. Her refusal to give up her seat on a Montgomery, Alabama city bus in 1955 started an American civil rights revolution. Her decision to choose wisdom helped to change a nation.

Such stories are all around us. Consider Ruth Nickels, a police officer in Alaska who lost her right arm in a ranching accident in 1990. Although it was difficult to cope with the loss of her arm, she refused to become dependent. Through grit and determination she taught herself the skills needed to survive as an amputee in an area of the country that is one of the most challenging anywhere. For years after her accident she provided inspiration to other amputees struggling to cope with limb loss.[4]

What do Rosa Parks, Nate Larkin and Ruth Nickels have in common? They each made a wise decision. They refused to accept the circumstances they had been dealt, and instead they each decided that they were not beyond hope, beyond improvement. They made a wise decision. And that decision changed their lives.

Regardless of where you are in life, where you are from, or what you've done, wisdom is available for you. Yes, it's available to everyone. But, you must decide to take wisdom up on her offer. And in order to do this, you must believe that your choices matter. You must believe that your choices do make a difference.

Whether you are behind a desk in a corner office or behind bars in a maximum-security prison, whether you consider yourself lucky or down on your luck, your choices matter. Wisdom is not just something available for the other guy—for someone else. Don't think you are beyond help, or beyond benefit. You can take advantage of wisdom's offer.

Not everyone can build a ministry, start a non-profit organization, or spark a political movement. But today, you can take wisdom up on her offer and start to make wise decisions. And wisdom does have its benefits, as we'll see in the coming chapters. Wisdom's benefits are available for you! Turn the pages of this book and discover how divine wisdom can change your life.

**Principle: Wisdom is available to everyone.**

**Life Lesson: You exercise wisdom by an act of the will. You can choose to be wise.**

# 2

# YOU MUST BE TEACHABLE

Greatness is rarely, if ever, inherent. Whether in sports, business, politics, entertainment, or any other field of endeavor, those that excel to the level of greatness do so because of a combination of talent, commitment, will, determination and hard work. In addition to raw talent, it takes discipline, consistency in training, and a willingness to learn from others. In these *uber*-competitive times, talent alone can get you only so far. Commitment and hard work are also essential. But, greatness comes through learning to apply expertise from those whose experience exceeds yours.

Ask anyone on the professional golf tour and they will tell you that during his prime, no one worked out harder in the weight room and practiced more than Tiger Woods. *Really? Wasn't he naturally talented?* Yes he is talented, but he also added to his talent a work ethic that was extraordinary. Former Seattle Seahawks Hall of Fame wide receiver Steve Largent used to spend hours *after* the Seahawks' practices running pass patterns— just to ensure that his footwork on his pass routes was precise. He didn't have the fastest time in the 40-yard dash (a standard measure of speed in the NFL), but he practiced his foot placement in order to run his pass routes with unparalleled precision. It was one of the reasons NFL cornerbacks found him so difficult to cover. These two world-class athletes knew that they were good, but they were also committed to *learning how* to improve. And, they were committed to *working hard* to improve. If that kind of talent is combined with both a commitment to learn and a commitment to work, the very talented can become great.

Greatness in sports doesn't come easy. Neither does becoming wise. Human nature—our natural tendency—is to think we can do things on our own. Our society tells us to become self-sufficient. To be needy, even to want or need advice, is universally judged as a sign of weakness. However, the truth is just the opposite. In order to be wise, you must become teachable— and not just teachable, but *ultra-teachable.*

In the last chapter we discussed that the first step to becoming wise is to recognize that *each of us has the capacity to become wise.* If we decide we want to become wise, we can. But the next step is *to be willing to be taught how* to become wise. Being *willing to be taught* is the key. You must first be willing to accept the fact that in and of yourself, you don't have the answer. You must be willing to admit that you need someone outside yourself to assist you. Being willing to be taught is foundational for obtaining wisdom and living a life of success. Proverbs has much to say about this.

To be wise, you have to be willing to accept both advice (which can be rewarding and encouraging) and correction (which is rarely a pleasant thing to endure) from other people. You must be willing to receive instruction, teaching and advice as a father teaches a son or an instructor teaches a student. But, you must also be willing to accept instruction specifically directed toward improving the things that you have done incorrectly, inaccurately, or just plain wrong. It's one thing to get instructions before starting an endeavor, but it takes a higher degree of humility and patience to receive correction on your mistakes. This is the type of correction described in Proverbs 9:8-9:

Do not reprove a scoffer, or he will hate you;
reprove a wise man, and he will love you.
Give instruction to a wise man, and he will be still wiser;
teach a righteous man, and he will increase in learning.

The central idea expressed here is that the wise man recognizes the value of correction. *If you want to be wise, you must choose not to be offended by correction.* The key is realizing that it is in your own best interest to be taught and corrected. So don't personalize the criticism. The purpose of reproof—genuine reproof—is not to make you feel bad about yourself but to help improve your performance. This is why a wise man welcomes correction. This principle is discussed repeatedly in Proverbs.

If you sit down over coffee with successful people, you'll find that few people who have achieved success have done so without help from others. Many successful people owe their success to mentors who have corrected them when necessary. Many, many successful people credit teachers and mentors who have had to take them aside and point out their warts and flaws, not for the purpose of insulting them, but to help them become the best that they can be. These mentors saw something in their younger protégés that caused them to invest into their lives and correct them, even at the risk of alienating them. They invested their energy and time to mentor them to a higher level of accomplishment.

Many know that Warren Buffett is considered to be the most successful investor in U.S. history. But Warren Buffett didn't become an investment expert by osmosis. Benjamin Graham mentored him for years beginning at Columbia University. Bill Gates, as founder of Microsoft, became the world's richest man. But he was schooled and challenged for years by his boss Dr. Ed Roberts, whom he credits as his mentor. Steve Jobs is known as one of the pre-eminent outside the box thinkers the tech world has ever seen. But he too had a mentor, Robert Friedland, who had a profound impact on him. As Jobs said, Friedland "turned me on to a different level of consciousness."[5]

You get the idea. Greatness doesn't happen naturally or easily. It usually involves tapping the skill and experience of mentors. Those that have gone

> Greatness doesn't happen naturally or easily. It usually involves tapping the skill and experience of mentors.

before us have much to teach us. And those willing to humble themselves and listen to correction stand to benefit much from the experiences of others.

The opposite is true also. If you do not accept correction and instruction from others, you are entering into an area that is common to failure. And that is putting it politely. In more common terms, those that refuse to listen to others are in for a very hard time. Proverbs has much to say about this:

> Whoever heeds instruction is on the path to life,
> but he who rejects reproof leads others astray.
> (Prov. 10:17)
>
> But he who hates reproof is stupid. (Prov. 12:1b)
>
> He who is often reproved, yet stiffens his neck,
> will suddenly be broken beyond healing. (Prov. 29:1)

In other words, you are stubborn at your own peril. If you will not accept reproof you will, in time, fail. You and I must acknowledge that we need advice and even correction, that we don't have the answers. We all have blind spots. And just as the side mirror on your car helps you see into your blind spots, so a mentor allows you to see what you cannot on your own—that

> If you will not accept reproof you will, in time, fail.

ugly, annoying part of your personality or those oft repeated mistakes in your performance or flaws in your personality or behavior that keep you from being your best.

One of the most poignant examples in history of refusing to be teachable and listen is Adolf Hitler's refusal to listen to his generals such as Field Marshall Walter von Brauchitsch, who was among the chorus of generals pleading with Hitler not to open a two-front war by invading Russia in June 1941. And once Hitler insisted on invading Russia, he would not let his Generals invade directly to Moscow. Instead, he insisted on taking Ukraine in the south. Many historians believe that this decision to open a two-front war was such a colossal error that it sealed Germany's fate. Despite having no command experience in battle, the German tyrant disregarded the advice of his military commanders. And it cost him everything. Proverbs repeats this principle throughout its pages.

> For by wise guidance you can wage your war,
> and in abundance of counselors there is victory.
> (Prov. 24:6)

> Whoever isolates himself seeks his own desire;
> he breaks out against all sound judgment.

> A fool takes no pleasure in understanding,
> but only in expressing his opinion. (Prov. 18:1-2)

> Like a gold ring or an ornament of gold
> is a wise reprover to a listening ear. (Prov. 25:12)

To become wise, you must acknowledge that you need wisdom, that you don't have life's answers in and of yourself. Think about this: you are the only person that

**You are the only person that will prevent you from becoming wise.**

will prevent you from becoming wise. Meditate on that for a moment. You are often your worst enemy. If you won't listen to others, then you are often working against yourself. Pretty humbling, isn't it?

Pride can prevent you from becoming wise. To become wise, you must be willing to take advice from others.

**Principle: You must be teachable.**

**Life Lesson: Humble yourself and be willing to learn.**

# 3

# YOU MUST LISTEN

While this may sound repetitive, this is not the same as being willing to be teachable and assuming a posture of humility.

Once you are willing to be taught, you must actually *learn to listen*. Yes, you must make an effort to listen, but you must also *learn to listen*. Listening is actually a skill that must be developed. Anyone can hear. But not everyone listens. Effective listening is one of the most overlooked skills a person possesses. It is a skill one can develop. And it is one of the most valuable skills *you* can develop.

It is one of the most important and repeated principles found throughout the book of Proverbs. Again and again we are told to listen:

Let the wise hear and increase in learning. (Prov. 1:5a)

Hear, my son, your father's instruction. (Prov. 1:8a)

Hear, O sons, a father's instruction, and be attentive, that you may gain insight (Prov. 4:1)

Hear, my son, and accept my words (Prov. 4:10a)

Give attention, incline your ear. (4:10)

Incline your ear to my understanding (Prov. 5:1b)

And now, O sons, listen to me, (Prov. 5:7a)

And now, O sons, listen to me,
and be attentive to the words of my mouth. (Prov. 7:24)

Listen (Prov. 8:6)

The Hebrew word for "listen" in these passages is *"shama"* and it means to hear intelligently, or to listen attentively. In other words, you must make an effort to understand and process what you are hearing. Listening is one of the most important skills you can develop, and it is one of the indispensable keys to finding wisdom. You see, it's not what you think you hear that matters— what matters is what is *actually being said.* And if you learn to listen—to really listen—it will amaze you what people will tell you.

Listening is not a passive activity. It requires that you suspend your ideas, your thoughts, set them aside in order to observe what is being communicated. There are quite sophisticated courses taught on learning to listen. Listen for main ideas. Listen for details. Listen for what is *not* being said. Listen for *how* it is being said and understand the context in which it is being said.

Intelligence officers are taught to use their powers of observation to summarize details quickly. Sometimes lives depend upon their observations. Law enforcement officers acknowledge that criminal investigations rely, and often pivot, on effective observation by witnesses. Development of observation skills is key to a police officer's effectiveness. His or her life may depend upon it. Every time a police officer pulls over an automobile or knocks on a suspect's door, his or her life is dependent upon the ability to observe the little things that appear out of the ordinary, such as the odor coming from the car, how the suspect is postured behind the wheel, or sounds coming from inside an apartment. These officers understand that true listening takes conscious effort.

Proverbs tells us to be quick to listen. The failure to listen is actually to disregard what is being communicated. Often, we disregard what others are saying because we have our own opinion. In your head, you hear your spouse say "x," and as the words come out of his/her mouth, you may be disregarding them because:

1. You think you know what he/she is already going to say;

2. You disagree with his/her opinion; or

3. You don't understand why he/she feels so strongly about the issue at hand.

Does this sound familiar? In short, we don't listen because we are thinking about how we will respond to what we think the other person is saying or is going to say.

This is not listening. This is barely tolerating the opinions of others. To listen, you must set aside your thoughts and actively attempt to understand what is being said, and why it is being said. This is active listening. It requires that we use our full power of observation that involves our ears, our eyes, and all our senses. Observe what is being communicated. Sometimes words even contradict what another person's body language is telling us. Listening is more than just using our ears.

> To listen, you must set aside your thoughts and actively attempt to understand what is being said, and why it is being said.

One of the most well-known examples of a failure to listen is the fateful disregarding of the warning telegraphs that were received aboard the *Titanic* during the second week of April 1912. On April 11, the *Titanic* received six ice warnings by Morse code from ships passing ahead of it through its projected route. There were five more warnings received on the 12th. Three more warnings were received on the

13th, and seven more on the 14th, the date of the fateful catastrophe. Three additional warnings were broadcast from the crow's nest to the bridge fifteen minutes before the ship struck the iceberg.[6] The ship wasn't just Captain Edward John Smith's responsibility. It was that of his entire team. He wasn't necessarily negligent. He did not receive some of the warnings. Others he minimized. Others he did receive and noted with caution. But in the end, he didn't give them the attention they deserved. He didn't use his full powers of observation, and he didn't engage his entire team to collectively utilize their combined listening skills. If he would have, things may have been different. One could imagine the conversation: *"Let's see, no moon, a calm, still night with no wind, we've had over 20 iceberg warnings, we're going much too fast... maybe we should slow down."*

> Those who won't listen don't really have a chance at becoming a wise person.

If you want to be wise, you must become an effective listener. Those who won't listen don't really have a chance at becoming a wise person. They are what the Bible refers to as the opposite. They will be what the Bible refers to as a fool.

**Principle: You must listen.**

**Life Lesson: You must learn to listen.
Practice becoming a good listener.**

# 4

# YOU MUST SEEK WISDOM

Finally, if you want to be wise, you must recognize the value of wisdom. You must recognize that wisdom is worth seeking. You must seek it, not just to find it, but also to *find it in order to apply it to your decisions.* Take note of Proverbs 2:1-5:

> My son, if you receive my words and treasure up my commandments with you, making your ear attentive to wisdom and inclining your heart to understanding; yes, if you call out for insight and raise your voice for understanding, if you seek it like silver and search for it as for hidden treasures, then you will understand the fear of the LORD and find the knowledge of God.

Also note Proverbs 4:7:

> The beginning of wisdom is this: Get wisdom,
> and whatever you get, get insight.

Notice the verbs in these passages: accept, store up, turn your ear, apply, call out for, cry aloud for, look for, search for, get. These are all action verbs. This is not a passive exercise. Obtaining wisdom won't happen by osmosis. It won't come naturally. Or easily. Wisdom doesn't come to the passive, or to the lazy. You must make a conscious effort to make wise choices. In fact, you must do more than make a conscious effort: you must actively pursue it. You must become a seeker of wisdom.

A great example of a seeker is Mel Fisher, often considered the world's greatest treasure hunter. Mel Fisher's dreams and aspirations began as a child when he read *Treasure Island* by Robert Louis Stevenson. In 1969 he began looking for the wreck of the Spanish galleon *Nuestra Senora de Atocha*. His search would become an obsession, eventually causing him to relocate his family to Key West, Florida, in order to facilitate his dream of finding the lost vessel. The search would take years. Then the years turned into decades. Despite the many setbacks, he is known for repeating every morning "today's the day." On July 20, 1985, sixteen years after he began his quest for the *Nuestra Senora de Atocha*, he found her. He found the wreck of the Spanish galleon that he had been looking for those many years, and her cargo certainly wasn't a disappointment. His haul of gold and silver came to about forty tons with a street value of over $400 million.[7]

Why did Mel Fisher find his Spanish galleon? Because he sought it, because after he couldn't find it, he didn't give up the search. He literally sought after her as one searches for a hidden treasure.

If you seek wisdom—really seek it, you will find it. In Proverbs 8:17 Wisdom calls,

> I love those who love me, and those who seek me diligently find me. (Prov. 8:17)

The primary reason we don't acquire wisdom is that we're not seeking it. To seek to make wise decisions is what Proverbs describes as "treasuring wisdom." How do you "treasure" wisdom? How does this work? There are three simple components, the first being the most important. The first component is the *attempt* to make a wise decision. The attempt is the key. It is *in the attempt* that you are seeking wisdom. Once you apply wisdom and make a decision, then the second component is evaluating your decision. Your willingness and ability to evaluate your actions are important because you must be able to understand why a decision was wise or unwise. What was the result? Who was impacted?

> The primary reason we don't acquire wisdom is that we're not seeking it.

Finally, the third component: when you have made a determination that a decision was wise or unwise, you should memorialize it in some way. Some, myself included, find that a journal is the simplest way to do this. Journaling helps you remember the event and look back upon it to help you make wise decisions in the future. This simple three-step process is one of the ways you can apply what Proverbs refers to as "treasuring wisdom."

1. Attempt.

2. Evaluate.

3. Memorialize.

Practice this simple process. When you find wisdom and begin the process of treasuring it, you are literally following the example of Mel Fisher. You are seeking after wisdom. You are seeking after it as one would a treasure. And it is appropriate that you do this because you see, the Scriptures describe wisdom as more valuable than gold and silver in Proverbs 8:18-21:

Riches and honor are with me,
  enduring wealth and righteousness.
My fruit is better than gold, even fine gold,
  and my yield than choice silver.
I walk in the way of righteousness,
  in the paths of justice,
granting an inheritance to those who love me,
  and filling their treasuries.

*Are you serious? Can I really become rich by pursuing wisdom?* I do not believe Proverbs describes a "get rich" formula. But, taken in the proper context, Proverbs 8:18-21 describes the fruit of a lifetime of wise decisions as all-inclusive: honor, a good reputation, and yes, material gain. The key is to understand this truth in the proper context, being the result of a lifetime, or an extended season of wise decisions.

How do we search for wisdom as if we were searching for treasure? Actively look for ways to apply wisdom. Learn to apply it. Learn to use it. Practice it. Attempt. Evaluate. Memorialize. And practice, practice, practice. In fact, Proverbs says, "doing wisdom is like sport to the wise man." In other words, the wise man practices making wise choices just for the buzz he gets out of doing it, out of knowing that he's doing something wise and the satisfaction he gets from knowing that he's moving toward wisdom.

What does it look like to practice wisdom? That's what the next twenty-four chapters are about. Turn the page, and let's get started.

**Principle: You must seek wisdom.**

**Life Lesson: Seeking wisdom means learning to apply
it and practice, practice, practice.**

PART II

# THE POWER OF WORDS

# 5

# WORDS ARE THE
# MOST POWERFUL TOOL
# IN YOUR LIFE

**W**ords spoken to us have power. They have the power to give us hope. To inspire. To motivate. To convey purpose. To make us laugh. To convey forgiveness. To convey joy. To restore. To reconcile. To heal. Words spoken in love are words of life. They are life giving. Proverbs tells us:

> Death and life are in the power of the tongue. (Prov. 18:21)

Death and life are in the power of the tongue.
(Prov. 18:21)

The mouth of the righteous is a fountain of life,
but the mouth of the wicked conceals violence.
(Prov. 10:11)

A gentle tongue is a tree of life,
but perverseness in it breaks the spirit. (Prov. 15:4)

Former Supreme Court Justice Oliver Wendell Holmes once described words as "the skin of a living thought."[8] This is a very accurate description because words convey powerful ideas.

The spoken word can also be destructive. In fact, negative words are the most destructive tool ever wielded against another human being. I want to repeat that; negative words—words spoken with malicious intent—are the most destructive tool ever wielded against another human being. Bombs and bullets can destroy the flesh, but words destroy the body, the soul and the spirit. You see, words extinguish hope. Words that wound can take one's will to live, drive us to despair and even to self-destruction. No physical weapon can do that. Hurtful words can destroy us. And your words can destroy the ones you love. Let me repeat that: Your words can destroy the ones you love.

> Negative words are the most destructive tool ever wielded against another human being.

How many times do we see this in our lives, and in the lives of those around us? A dear friend of mine told me of meeting a man named Roger, whose life demonstrated this principle all too vividly. Upon meeting Roger, it was evident that he had a very low self-esteem. He wouldn't look a person in the eye when he was spoken to. His handshake was feeble.

> Your words can destroy the ones you love.

His lack of confidence was apparent. When my friend met Roger, his first impression was that he was a little boy in a grown man's body. As my friend got to know Roger, he learned he had had difficulty in holding a job throughout his life. He also learned that his wife complained bitterly that he never provided his children with the nurture they needed. Only when my friend met Roger's mother did his behavior make sense. Roger's mother exuded disapproval toward her son. She offered few, if any, kind words to Roger. My friend later found out that most of her communication with her son throughout his life had consisted of criticism. From her perspective, Roger could do nothing right. From Roger's perspective, he could never live up to her expectations. Everything he did was insufficient. Sadly, Roger lived to earn her approval, which of course, he never would obtain. Roger has been shaped and molded by decades of criticism and ridicule. Words from a disapproving mother have destroyed him.

Dr. Christiane Northrup, a practicing family physician and author, echoes the profound impact a mother's words can have on her children, particularly her daughters:

> A mother's often unconscious influence on her daughter's health is so profound that years ago I had to accept that my medical skills were only a drop in the bucket compared to the unexamined and ongoing influence of her mother. If a woman's relationship with her mother was supportive and healthy, and if her mother had given her positive messages about her female body and how to care for it, my job as a physician was easy. If on the other hand, her mother's influence was problematic, or if there was a history of neglect, abuse, alcoholism or mental illness, then I knew that my best efforts would probably fall short. Real long-term health solutions would become possible *only* when my patient realized the impact of her background and then took steps to change this influence.[9]

A father's impact is also profound. The late Michael Jackson's estranged relationship with his father, Joe Jackson, is well known. As a child, Michael was driven hard by his father to develop his obvious musical and dancing talent, to the point of being denied a normal childhood. It was a major reason why in later years Jackson so loved his 3,000-acre, Peter Pan-inspired Never Land Ranch, nestled near Santa Barbara, California, with its carnival-style rides and amusements. By his own account, Michael's relationship with his father was void of affection. Michael said he was never permitted to call him "Father" or "Dad," but always "Joseph." A sensitive child, Jackson revealed in his 1988 autobiography that his father regularly beat him and that "just a look would scare you." The emotional abuse deeply affected Michael, as the world would come to see in later years.[10]

> "I was so shy I would wash my face in the dark," Michael once told Oprah Winfrey, referring to an acne outbreak he experienced as a child. "I wouldn't look in the mirror, and my father teased me. I just hated it. I would cry every day. He would tell me I'm ugly."

When he died in 2009, it was disclosed that Michael Jackson, in his will, had left nothing of his remaining (or future) fortune to 80-year-old Joseph Jackson, the man at the center of the Jackson family, who had pushed his son Michael into the entertainment stratosphere, while crushing him privately with his demands, words, and actions.

Craig McConnell's story is one that more of us can relate to. His father was killed in the Korean War and his mother remarried when he was three. His stepfather's impact upon him was profound. He made it a habit of telling young Craig, "You are nothing but a seagull... you are only good for sitting, squatting and (defecating)." Craig believed him. Craig recalls that in his mind, he believed, "I have absolutely nothing to offer... I sit, squawk and (defecate). Period." Craig really believed he had nothing to contribute. No value and no purpose. These thoughts became ingrained in him as a young boy and formed the parameters by which he defined himself and his existence. So his adolescent years were marked by aimless wanderings to find out where he fit. It took decades, but he eventually was able to break free from these destructive ideas imposed upon him as a young boy.

As an adult, he finally discovered the truth: that he is uniquely crafted in the image of his Creator, that he is of infinite worth and value, and that he is indeed gifted for many, many things. Breaking free from the destructive power of those words spoken over him as a child has been a lifelong challenge. But he eventually was set free from this destructive influence. For several years before his death in 2016, Craig helped others find freedom through Ransomed Heart, a writing and teaching ministry based in Colorado Springs, Colorado.[11]

Yes, words have power, and because words are so powerful, you must learn to choose the right words in appropriate ways. Think about this idea for a moment: You don't keep combustible chemicals near your food pantry. Why? Because you don't want to inadvertently consume or mix the wrong ingredients. The consequences could be disastrous. Likewise, you must choose very carefully—both the words you use, and how you use them.

Proverbs 25:11 reads:

A word fitly spoken is like apples of gold in a setting
of silver.

Proverbs 15:23 also affirms the importance of careful words:

To make an apt answer is a joy to a man,
and a word in season, how good it is!

Words can accomplish almost anything. The spoken word can inspire, encourage and entertain. We see this every day in magnificent works of literature and the arts. We see those such as Abraham Lincoln or Winston Churchill, who were able to weave together words in ways that inspire a nation; or others make us laugh like Garrison Keiler, Robin

> Words can accomplish almost anything.

Williams, Dana Carvey or countless others. Poets, playwrights and authors understand this powerful principle. Proverbs challenges us to take it to heart as well.

Ken Blanchard, who conducts business training seminars all over America, tells an inspiring story of a young man who taught an entire community of the power of encouraging words. In his book *The Simple Truths of Service*, he tells the story of Johnny the Bagger. Johnny was a nineteen-year-old boy with Downs Syndrome who bagged groceries at a local grocery store. Johnny had attended one of Blanchard's seminars on customer service that explained the power that words hold in people's lives. After the seminar, Johnny contacted Blanchard's office and related his story. He said,

> I went back to the store and I didn't know how to apply your statements. I liked your talk but I didn't know what to do with it. I went home and talked with my dad and got an idea. My dad and I sat down at the computer and every day we come up with a statement that is affirming of people, that's encouraging. If I can't find one in a little quote book, I'll make it up. We'll type it up six different times on the computer. I print off fifty sheets and cut all of them.[12]

Then, every night, Johnny would personally sign each of roughly 300 quotes. Then the next day at the grocery store he put the stack of quotes next to the spot where he bagged the groceries. In each customer's last sack he put the quote of the day, the encouraging word. He made sure he looked them in the eye and said, "I put something very special for you in this sack. I hope it will brighten your day." He took the customer out to their car and helped them load up. Johnny did this every single day.

About a month later, the manager of that grocery store contacted Blanchard's office. He said, "I can't believe it. Something really amazing is beginning to happen. I was walking around the store and I noticed while we had lots of checkers at the checkout line, there was no one there but maybe one or two people. The line where Johnny was doing bagging went all the way back to the frozen food section." True story! He said:

> I would tell them over the intercom that there were other lines you could move over to. We would walk down the line and tell people there were other lines open. People would just look at us and say, "No, we'll wait because we want Johnny's encouraging word for the day." One woman came by and grabbed the supervisor. She said, "I used to only come to the grocery store once a week or once every other week. Now I come by almost every day. I buy something just so I can get Johnny's encouraging word for the day."

About a month later, the store manager called Blanchard's office and said,

> It's changing our entire culture of our store. Even in the floral department when a flower was broken they used to just throw it away. Now they walk out into the lines, on their own initiative, they pin it onto elderly women or young girls. They brighten their day. Listen, there are a lot of people in the organizational chart at that grocery store but I'm telling you the most important person is Johnny, the bagger. He's speaking words of life and words of life can change a culture.

What a vivid example of the power of words.

One day, your life will end, and you will be gone. The only part of you that will remain on this earth is the memory of you and the impact that you have had on others. Only the actions you've taken and the words you have spoken to others will remain. If something happened to you today, and those close to you were required to summarize your life based upon your impact upon them thus far, based upon the words you have spoken to them, what would they say about you?

> How have your words impacted those closest to you?

What would they say? How have your words impacted those closest to you?

If you want to be wise, you must understand and incorporate into your daily life, the power of words.

**Principle: Words are the most powerful tool in your life.**

**Life Lesson: Recognize the power of words, and choose your words carefully.**

# 6

# GUARD YOUR WORDS

Chapter 5 focused on the need to choose our words carefully—to choose *which* words we use. This chapter warns us to limit the shear amount of words we use. This is a subtle, but very important distinction. Proverbs repeatedly warns against talking too much. This may sound overly simple, but it is, I believe, one of the most ignored fundamental behaviors of civilized society, and it is a profound truth that must be applied to your life if you want to walk in wisdom. These references are repeated warnings about being a motor mouth.

> When words are many, transgression is not lacking,
> but whoever restrains his lips is prudent. (Prov. 10:19)

> Whoever guards his mouth preserves his life;
> he who opens wide his lips comes to ruin. (Prov. 13:3)

> Whoever keeps his mouth and his tongue
> keeps himself out of trouble. (Prov. 21:23)

> Do you see a man who is hasty in his words?
> There is more hope for a fool than for him. (Prov. 29:20)

Even a fool who keeps silent is considered wise;
   when he closes his lips, he is deemed intelligent.
   (Prov. 17:28)

Both Abraham Lincoln and early American author Mark Twain
have been credited with this humorous spin on this important
truth of Proverbs 17:28:

It is better to keep your mouth closed and let people
think you are a fool than to open it and remove all
doubt.[13]

So Chatty Kathy's beware. You need to learn to close your
mouth. When you run across someone that doesn't apply this
principle, it really stands out. I remember standing in line for
a movie a few years back. It was opening weekend for a major
summer blockbuster, and after we had purchased our tickets we
had to stand in line in order to get a good seat. While we were
in line, we couldn't help but overhear a young couple behind us.
They were a well-dressed, attractive couple, but I noticed that the
young man had a nervous energy about him because he wouldn't
stop talking. At first it just appeared that maybe he had had too
much coffee or perhaps too much sugar. Then it became apparent
that he had a serious problem. He spoke so much, and so fast that
he literally didn't stop. He didn't stop talking for ten minutes,
and it wasn't a two-way conversation between him and his female
friend. It wasn't one description of a detailed event. It wasn't
a conversation at all. It was one continuous non-stop rambling
from topic to topic without much of a breath in between. It was
one long, uninterrupted sentence about his ideas, his opinions,
his concerns, and his views. He didn't stop talking the entire time
we were in line. As he continued to speak, the irony was evident;
the more he spoke, the less credibility he retained. The more he
spoke, the less he was worth listening to. It was as if he was dem-
onstrating to those around him how little he really had to say. At

first, the topic of his conversation was just small talk. But as he proceeded, it was apparent that the topic of his conversation was nothing more than a rambling string of opinions. After several minutes, it didn't even rate as trivial. It had eroded into babble.

By the time we were walking into the theatre, I couldn't wait to get as far away from him as possible. This man was one of the most annoying people I have ever been around. If he would have just stopped talking, he would have appeared as a half decent guy. But he was his own worst enemy. His incessant talking was literally driving people away from him. I felt sorry for the girl that was with him. He would have been well served to have taken Mark Twain's advice.

A wise person speaks little and listens much. Guard your words. Be slow to speak.

**Principle: Guard your words.**

**Life Lesson: Don't talk too much.**

# 7

# GOSSIP DESTROYS PEOPLE

G ossip destroys people. Proverbs is unmistakably clear on this topic:

Whoever covers an offense seeks love,
> but he who repeats a matter separates close friends.
> (Prov. 17:9)

Whoever goes about slandering reveals secrets;
> therefore do not associate with a simple babbler.
> (Prov. 20:19)

The words of a whisperer [gossip] are like delicious
> morsels;
> they go down into the inner parts of the body.
> (Prov. 26:22)

Put away from you crooked speech,
> and put devious talk far from you. (Prov. 4:24)

Whoever goes about slandering reveals secrets,
> but he who is trustworthy in spirit keeps a thing
> covered. (Prov. 11:13)

What is gossip? The dictionary defines gossip as:

- Idle talk or rumor, especially about the personal or private affairs of others.

- Conversation about personal matters: conversation about the personal details of other people's lives, whether rumor or fact, especially when malicious.

- A conversation between two people that concerns a third person who is not present.

- Talking about the private concerns of other people. (Dictionary.com)

Wow! That sounds like what you hear every day from people all around you, doesn't it? If that is gossip, then its everywhere, isn't it? Yes it is. And it's pretty easy to do. Gossip is so prevalent in our culture that we become de-sensitized to it. It happens all the time. Everywhere. It's even celebrated in magazines, websites and tabloid TV shows.

Our culture doesn't see the harm in gossip. It is often seen as a generally accepted pastime when we congregate in the office around the water cooler, in the lunchroom or around the coffee maker. Proverbs, however, instructs not to associate with people who gossip.

So how do you recognize gossip when you hear it? How do you know if you are gossiping? To know if you are gossiping about someone, you might ask yourself how you would feel if the person being talked about walked into the room to hear what was being said about him or her. Another test is to ask yourself if your conversation were recorded, would you (and others) be able to listen to your conversation without being embarrassed? Or, if a transcript of your conversation appeared in the newspaper or online, would you be embarrassed by your participation in it?

Gossip is easy to do. In fact, you don't even have to repeat it to participate. Just by listening to gossip you feed it, and you allow it to affect you. Think about it; once you've heard negative juicy gossip about someone, can you just easily put that out of your mind? Not really. Your view of them is tainted or at the very minimum shaded in one way or another. What Proverbs refers to as "whispers" go down deep. They have a deep impact upon how we view others.

Gossip is dangerous on many levels. Gossip hurts others. Gossip is not fair. It unjustly accuses someone without them being able to defend themselves. Gossip is speculative. Gossip is not accountable. Gossip excludes people. Gossip destroys trust in others. It is destructive.

Gossip in the workplace has always been problematic, but in recent years, the immediacy of information available via the Internet and the ability to pass information along via social media has allowed gossip to spread exponentially faster than ever before. Author Samuel Greengard tells a story of Marie, a young woman driven from her job at an insurance company because of vicious, unfounded rumors in the workplace of her sexual preferences. Marie,

> Stepped into her cubicle at a major insurance company and overheard her coworkers buzzing about her sex life over coffee and doughnuts. As the discussion about her sexual preferences seeped through the partition walls, she cringed and recoiled in horror. The fact that the rumor was false contributed to only part of her feelings of embarrassment, betrayal, and degradation. "It's even worse that your character is destroyed in front of the entire company," Marie said, "There is no way to describe how awful it is to become the object of company ridicule. I wanted to disappear and never come back. I felt like I was wearing a scarlet letter." On that rainy November morning, the 32-year-old single woman re-

alized that the gloom outside the office window was nothing compared to how she felt inside. During the following weeks, her hurt and anger mounted and her productivity declined. Rather than denying that she was a "dyke," as they had referred to her, she quietly shuffled papers and did the best she could to trudge through her work and get through the day. Three months after the incident, she quit the job and found a place to work where she was treated with dignity and respect.[14]

An often-repeated humorous story about Winston Churchill shows how ridiculous and embarrassing gossip can be for those engaging in it:

Winston Churchill exemplified integrity and respect in the face of opposition. During his last year in office, he attended an official ceremony. Several rows behind him two gentlemen began whispering. "That's Winston Churchill." "They say he is getting senile." "They say he should step aside and leave the running of the nation to more dynamic and capable men." When the ceremony was over, Churchill turned to the men and said, "Gentlemen, they also say he is deaf!"[15]

It is not known if this story is accurate, but it if is, think of how foolish these two individuals must have felt. They were fortunate enough to have been able to briefly encounter one of history's most renowned leaders, one of the true giants of the twentieth century. What an honor. But rather than have him greet you and say, "Nice to meet you," he essentially turns to you and says (with justification) "You're an idiot." Kind of hard to pass that story on to one's grandkids, eh?

Here's another quote that is highly appropriate, but its source is unknown:

- People of high intelligence talk about ideas.

- People of average intelligence talk about things.

- People of little intelligence talk about other people.

Where are you in this lineup?

You will never become wise if you do not understand the destructive power of gossip.

Proverbs instructs us on how to deal with gossip. It simply tells us not to participate. If you find yourself being told something about someone, then keep it to yourself. (This doesn't apply to information that may endanger other people. Of course, we all have a responsibility to convey information to authorities if that information regards safety and security

> You will never become wise if you do not understand the destructive power of gossip.

issues). When someone is gossiping, you don't have to participate. You don't have to be an audience. Whether by walking away or by vocally letting people know that you don't want to participate in gossip, you can make a rumor stop with you. Confronting such common behavior can be very awkward. When in awkward situations, I find the best course of action is to be honest. People appreciate authenticity. You might say something like, "I'm sorry, but I'm not comfortable talking about this person when they are not around." Again, when someone is gossiping, you don't have to participate.

If you want to be wise, you must leave behind the practice of gossip, and separate yourself from those that gossip.

**Principle: Gossip destroys people.**

**Life Lesson: Don't gossip.**

# PART III

# RELATIONSHIPS, FAMILY & SEX

# 8

# GUARD YOUR AFFECTIONS

Proverbs 4:23 states:

Keep your heart with all vigilance,
For from it flow the springs of life.

The Bible refers to the "heart" as affections. The Hebrew word used here for the word "heart" is *leb* (*labe*) and refers to feelings, will and intellect. This verse is warning the reader to watch over or guard (to be careful and selective) what (and who) you allow yourself to value. Be very careful in what and in whom you place your admiration, your devotion and your trust.

> Your affections... are your most important possessions.

Your affections—your admiration, trust and devotion, who and what you are willing to give to and sacrifice for—are the most valuable things you have. They are your most important possessions. Proverbs warns us to guard, or protect those possessions with *all* diligence. The people, ideas and objects that are the recipient of those precious possessions must be selected very carefully.

This principle applies to ideas, ideologies, and possessions, but most importantly it applies to people. To be blunt, you must be careful whom you allow yourself to fall for. If you want to be wise, be very selective to whom you give your affection.

One common theory of how we develop affection for others is that we are attracted to other people based upon factors such as their physical attractiveness, their closeness in proximity, their familiarity to us, or their similarity to us. Statistically, this theory plays out in practice, as most couples do share one or more similarities in age, location, race, religion and education. We tend to date and marry people that share our interests, or that we come into contact with through school, work or through social connections. So how we as a society select our mates is actually very practical.

But sometimes these considerations can become too practical for our own good. Too often, because of fear, anxiety, or dependency, many people settle for a relationship that is easy or practical, but may not be in their long-term best interest. How many people do you know that are with a partner, but you and others around them can't figure out why? "What does she see in him?" becomes the question that begs to be answered. After spending time around the couple you get the sense that your friend is settling for less than the ideal partner. Whether for convenience, or from fear of not finding a mate, they seem to settle for what is safe, convenient, or even just available.

I saw this several years ago, when my wife and I celebrated a wedding anniversary in the Caribbean. We were at a beautiful beachside resort. When we go to a resort, I like to lay out and relax to music, or read and enjoy the sun's rays while my wife prefers meeting people, talking with others and making new friends. The pool at the resort had a swim-up bar, so she spent hours there in the pool meeting people that congregated around the bar. She spent the afternoon talking with new acquaintances in the built-in chairs and the in-water chaise that was built into the pool. During one afternoon, we met a couple in their late forties, Don and Brenda. Talking privately with Brenda, Laurie told her that we were celebrating our wedding anniversary. Brenda suddenly became very quiet, looked down at the water, and, after an awkward silence, finally remarked that she had been with Don for ten years, but that, "Don won't marry me."

Laurie could tell that it was a difficult topic for Brenda. Laurie looked her directly in the eye and with all the tenderness she could muster, asked, "Then why do you stay with him?" You could tell from the look on her face that it was a question that pierced Brenda to the core. She thought for a moment, and finally she replied, "I don't know why I stay with him."

Laurie responded, "If he won't marry you, what does that say about how much value he places on you? Brenda, you are worth more than that."

Whether consciously or subconsciously, Brenda had settled. She had accepted what was convenient, what was familiar, what was safe. And the fruit of that decision was evident. Her reason for staying with Don wasn't "because he loves me, because I love him, because he's wonderful," or any other list of qualities she could have described. She couldn't answer. She literally didn't know and couldn't identify why she stayed with Don.

> Make sure those people and things that want your devotion, love and affection are worthy of them.

Do not settle for what is available, convenient, or easy. Make sure those people and things that want your devotion, love and affection are worthy of them. To settle for less is to compromise your values, to sell yourself short. In doing so, you forsake your authenticity and sacrifice your self-respect.

This is the conviction of Jen Schefft, one of the original contestants on ABC's *The Bachelor* television show. On the show, she rejected two different marriage proposals. She also dated another contestant, Andrew Firestone, heir to the tire-making fortune, but eventually she ended the relationship. Jen describes her decisions on these relationships as a refusal to settle. Schefft has written a relationship book for singles, *Better Single Than Sorry: A No-Regrets Guide to Loving Yourself and Never Settling.* Settling, she says, means being in a relationship that's less than you deserve, or that's not right for you, just for the sake of being in a relationship. She encourages women to, "be proud of yourself for having the courage not to settle."[16] Jen is thankful she didn't settle because she eventually found what she was looking for. Today, Jen lives in Illinois with her husband and two young girls.

There is another aspect to affection that deserves mentioning. When we make the decision to place our trust in something or someone and we give them our affection, the attraction process often rapidly escalates and can shift into fast forward. When we consciously place our trust and hope in someone or something, we become vulnerable because we are exposing parts of ourselves that are extremely personal, even intimate. And when that affection is reciprocated, even a little bit, it bonds us to that person quickly and often very strongly.

We develop attraction for things and people that meet a very personal need in our lives. It may be a desire or need to enjoy or possess beauty, or a need for validation, approval or esteem. And when those needs are met by the attention or affection of others, it is very significant, and it has a powerful effect upon us. Those people that we allow to meet those needs (or those that we think are meeting those needs) fill a special place in our "hearts" and the bonds that ensue are quite powerful. A woman's admiring look can, in an instant, affirm a man's feelings of masculinity. A man's tender word and gentle manner, or a glance and a tender expression can stir a woman's inner need for security, or make her feel that yes, she is indeed lovely.

This is why we can be so easily hurt in a romantic relationship. When we open our "hearts" to another and become vulnerable, we are exposing our most intimate and personal needs. Isn't it only logical that those people that receive that honor should be able to handle the responsibility?

Would you trust an amateur to mix your prescription medication, perform routine maintenance on a 747-jet airliner, or perform surgery on you or your child? Of course not! Only those that have demonstrated an ability, expertise, or competency should be allowed to perform those highly skilled functions. Yet, people every day open themselves to amateurs, fools, or those that lack character—people that don't have any business holding our most precious possessions in their hands. In order for someone to be trusted with your heart, he or she must earn that trust.

I know of a young woman, Shannon (pseudonym), who has had difficulty in romantic relationships. On the surface, one might say that she appears to be falling for the wrong men, or the wrong type of men. Shannon is extremely attractive and has no trouble attracting men. She has, in fact, had many, many boyfriends in the last ten years. But, three features mark her relationships; first, they seem to go very deep, very fast. Second, they do not last very long. Third, not long after each relationship is over, she is quickly and deeply involved in another one. So she has many "serious" relationships that do not last for a long period of time, and when they are over, she is quickly involved in another romantic relationship.

From knowing her, it's clear that Shannon wants to be in a romantic relationship, so much so that she imposes the model of "boyfriend relationship" on it from the start. So very quickly, the relationship goes deep, with all of the privileges and expectations that accompany that kind of relationship. In essence, Shannon is giving her heart away much too early. She immediately assumes that because a man expresses interest in her, that he is also capable of shouldering the responsibilities involved. She places her trust in him, shares her emotions with him, and sadly, showers him with her affections, only to find out within a short amount of time that he is not capable of handling such a responsibility. As a result, the last several years have seen a long series of failed relationships that have been characterized by unrealized expectations.

And Shannon wonders why all of the guys she dates are losers. Shannon hasn't applied what Proverbs shows us. She hasn't learned to watch over her heart with all diligence. She hasn't learned to guard her affections.

Another reason that we must learn to treasure, protect, and guard our affections is because those things and people that we allow ourselves to value and embrace willingly, will actually determine which types of things also tempt us.

The Scriptures repeat several times that a person's temptations (the things that tempt us) actually stem from one's own desires. The idea is that we are led astray by our own innermost desires. This sounds mysterious, but it is actually very practical. If we embrace something as valuable, assign value to it, or place our trust and devotion in it, then it has a degree of influence over us. This entity can shape our judgment, influence our perspective and impact our decision-making. It can be a good thing, such as repeatedly investing into a good relationship and seeing your love for that person grow over time, or it can have negative results. If for example, you repeatedly allow a manipulative person's behavior to go unchecked, they will eventually become dominant in an unhealthy way.

This is the nature of addiction. By repeatedly submitting our will and our choices to something that is unhealthy— whether an abusive person, or inanimate things such as food or chemicals—it will, at best, have disproportionate influence over us, or at worst, become dominant in our lives. Either way it will have an unhealthy power over us.

Ironically, this is the one proverb that Solomon himself failed to apply. He was wise, even possessing supernatural wisdom granted to him by God. But Solomon wasn't perfect. He was fallible. He struggled in this area so much that this failure is credited for bringing down his kingdom. As we have seen in previous chapters, Solomon lived large, rarely doing anything with half an effort. So in addition to his wisdom, wealth, leadership, civic progress in culture, science and poetry, and all of his other accomplishments, Solomon is also known for his many wives. He had a literal harem of 700 wives and 300 concubines. This sounds absurd to modern culture, but this was in a time when polygamy was common among kings, and the Jewish culture or Scripture hadn't yet prohibited it.

So as with everything else he did, Solomon took it to the limit. Many of his marriages were motivated by political and military alliances. You can imagine that foreign kings were often reluctant to conquer their neighbors if their grandkids were going to be among the victims. What at the time may have been considered brilliant political and military strategy, however, became Solomon's Achilles heel, because many of his foreign wives brought with them foreign religious practices, including idols and idol worship. These practices of his wives (and their children) became pervasive throughout the country and eroded both Solomon's and the Jewish peoples' commitment to following the Jewish religious law. There were entire neighborhoods of foreign-born women whose households (no doubt populated with Solomon's children) worshipped foreign idols.

Scripture condemns these foreign religious practices as the reason for the national religious decline that came after Solomon's death. Ironically, Solomon didn't follow his own advice. Had Solomon been able to do so, he might have preserved his nation. But, Solomon's failure to guard his affections was credited with the disintegration of his monarchial kingdom within just a few generations and ultimately would result in the nation being destroyed by the Babylonian empire four hundred years later.

The fact that he, as the wisest of the wise, fell victim to this danger is evidence of the challenges that face all of us in guarding our affections. It is evidence of just how difficult it is to apply everyday. How does one guard his or her affections? Proverbs 4: 25 provides a tip:

> "Let your eyes look directly forward, and your gaze be straight before you."

Proverbs is saying, in short, be careful of distractions and entice-ments. Our culture offers many of them, and they shouldn't be treated lightly or casually. In short, they are not something to mess with. Instead, Proverbs tells us to be intentional. Be focused. Realize that the things you allow yourself to partake in, the ide-ologies you adopt, and the people you pursue, will have a power-ful impact upon your eternal destiny. And as you are intent on pursuing wisdom, be intentional, be focused, and be diligent.

### Principle: Guard your affections.

### Life Lesson: Be selective with your affections. Be careful to what and to whom you give your heart.

# 9

# STAY AWAY FROM FOOLS

Proverbs 13:20 says that,

> Whoever walks with the wise becomes wise,
> but the companion of fools will suffer harm.

As we discussed in Chapter 5, our earliest and most lasting influences come from our parents and siblings. It is difficult to overestimate the value of these early bonds. Being raised in a nurturing family by loving and attentive parents and caregivers increases one's chances of developing healthy relationships as an adult. Conversely, a lack of a nurturing environment as a small child has a detrimental impact on a person's social development. And as you become older and move beyond these bonds of immediate family members to develop greater autonomy with whom you associate, the influence of your immediate family is gradually reduced, supplanted by the influence of your immediate friends.

Growing up, our close friends shape how we view ourselves and how we perceive those around us. For better or worse, they shape our attitudes and values. The influence our peers have upon us is profound, particularly as we are moving from childhood into adolescence. You've heard it since you were a child, but it really is true: those you run with heavily influence you. You pick up their habits. You start to talk like them, dress like them, think like them, believe like them, and act like them.

If you doubt this is true, think about the way we learn to speak as children. Dr. John Holt, in his book *How Children Learn*, points out that we rely on this principle so strongly that as a society, we don't even try to formally teach children to speak. If we did try to formally teach children to speak, he asks, how would we do it? Perhaps curriculum committees would analyze which speech skills were most important or drill young toddlers in certain speech skills. "Suppose we tried to do this?" he asks, "What would happen? What would happen, quite simply, is that most children, before they got very far, would become baffled, discouraged, humiliated, and fearful, and quit trying to do what we asked them."[17]

No, children don't learn to speak through formal education, but by listening to the language of their environment twenty-four hours a day, seven days a week. As they are immersed in a language, it becomes part of how they think, and consequently how they communicate. It works for any language and every language. If immersed in any specific language, a child will become fluent in that language by the age of five.

This is the principle conveyed in Proverbs regarding walking in close, constant companionship with fools. If you immerse yourself in the company of fools, you won't escape that environment without suffering the effects. And, there will be effects. If you walk in constant companionship with a fool, it will have a negative impact upon your life. That's why Proverbs 14:7 says, "Leave the presence of a fool."

> "Leave the presence of a fool."

Leave the presence of a fool,
    for there you do not meet words of knowledge.
    (Prov. 14:7)

But isn't this rather harsh? Isn't that just being a snob? Before we look at that question, we must first ask, "What is a fool?" Or more specifically, "What makes someone a fool?" Proverbs has a lot to say about fools, but the most often mentioned trait that characterizes a fool is that they don't listen to the advice of others. Just about all of Proverbs 26 expounds on the characteristic of a fool:

| Verse of Proverbs 26 | A fool: |
| --- | --- |
| [1] Like snow in summer or rain in harvest, <br> honor is not fitting for a fool. | Doesn't deserve honor |
| [3] A whip for the horse, a bridle for the donkey, <br> and a rod for the backs of fools! | Does things worthy of discipline |
| [6] Whoever sends a message by the hand of a fool cuts off his own feet and drinks violence. | Shouldn't be trusted to represent you |
| [7] Like a lame man's legs, which hang useless, <br> is a proverb in the mouth of fools. | Doesn't have credibility when they speak wisely |
| [8] Like one who binds the stone in the sling is one who gives honor to a fool. | Don't deserve honor |
| [10] Like an archer who wounds everyone is one who hires a passing fool or drunkard. | Can't be trusted with responsibility |
| [11] Like a dog that returns to his vomit, is a fool who repeats his folly. | Is habitually locked into his ways |

Because fools don't listen, it is very difficult to engage them in any form of meaningful, substantive discussion that involves controversy or conflict. You might as well argue with the wind. Proverbs 29:9 says,

> If a wise man has an argument with a fool,
>     the fool only rages and laughs, and there is no quiet.

The Message translates this verse as:

> A sage trying to work things out with a fool gets only scorn and sarcasm for his trouble. (The Message: the Bible in Contemporary Language)

Proverbs also characterizes a fool as someone who is quick to argue.

> It is an honor for a man to keep aloof from strife,
>     but every fool will be quarreling. (Prov. 20:3)

According to Proverbs a fool is also one who will engage in arguments that aren't their own, or in other words, one who participates in arguments that really aren't any of their business.

> Whoever meddles in a quarrel not his own
>     is like one who takes a passing dog by the ears.
>     (Prov. 26:17)

Several of the character traits that characterize a fool are connected to an attitude of pride. Proud people don't listen very well. They enjoy hearing themselves talk more than listening to others. Prideful people over value their opinion and undervalue the opinions of others. They don't take correction from others.

So if you know someone who refuses to listen to others, won't take correction from those around them, continually says things that have no credibility, who can't be trusted with responsibility, who always blames others for their problems, is overly quick to argue, and is prideful, do yourself a favor and follow the advice of Proverbs 14:7 and leave them alone:

> Leave the presence of a fool,
>> for there you do not meet words of knowledge.

So, back to our question: Isn't the instruction in 14:7 to leave the presence of a fool harsh? Isn't that just being a snob?

No it's not being a snob. You should be nice. You should be polite, but limit your involvement with fools. Don't hang out with them. Don't invest your valuable time with them. Also, resist the temptation to try to help them out of a sense of obligation or pity. Rather than helping them, you will end up having to loan them money or bail them out of a jam due to their poor decisions. You see, fools make foolish decisions. They make messes. And the friends of fools end up having to clean up their messes. Unless you want to clean up a mess, leave the presence of a fool.

But wait a minute, isn't it a good thing to try to help other people? Well some people, yes. But in the case of a fool, Proverbs, as you can see, is quite specific on this topic.

One of the reasons that Proverbs gives such a strong warning against hanging around with fools is that life is just too short, and your time is just too valuable to squander it on fools. This world is full of people who make very, very poor choices—people who have made a lifestyle of poor choices. Having such people as confidants—friends that influence you—is asking for trouble.

One thing that will help here is to learn to see your time as the valuable commodity that it is. This is one of the most common mistakes young people make. Young people often fail to understand the value of time. When you are young you have more time than money. Many people find that when they are old, they have more money than time. It is not until later in life that people truly realize that time is the most valuable commodity that they possess. You can always earn more money, but your time on earth is finite. Once your time is up, it's up. That's why it is important to invest your valuable time in quality relationships.

A wise person invests their valuable commodities and resources—their time and their money—in those things and in those people that will either benefit them or that will benefit others. When you invest in a relationship with a giving, loving person, you benefit from them, from the insight and wisdom they have to offer, from their caring compassion. In a mentoring relationship, most of the benefit is for the protégé that gleans wisdom or life skills from the mentor.

But spending a lot of time with fools is not productive or wise. You see, fools don't want to listen to others. They won't learn from the advice that others (including you) are willing to offer. They just take and take, and keep taking—as much as you'll give. They'll take your time. They'll take your money and your trust. They'll consume whatever you have.

Proverbs actually says that acting foolish by making unwise or even idiotic decisions is like sport to a fool (Prov. 10:23). They actually derive a sense of enjoyment from their behavior. There is no desire to change. This is why trying to reason with a fool can be like butting your head against a wall or arguing with the wind.

Thus, the admonitions from Proverbs 20:3:

> Keeping away from fools can help to keep you out of
> pointless arguments.

Likewise, Proverbs 22:24 warns:

> Make no friendship with a man given to anger,
> nor go with a wrathful man. (Prov. 22:24)

If these warnings apply to having fools as a close friend, then they *really* apply (with exclamation points!) to having a fool as a romantic interest. If you are in a serious romantic relationship with one that Proverbs would describe as a fool, flee that relationship immediately. The foolish behavior of this person will ensnare you with headache and with heartache.

Keep away from fools. I know, it's much easier to acknowledge than it is to apply. You may agree with it in theory, but are you able (or willing) to apply it? Avoiding trust relationships with fools is harder than it sounds. We see it in others all the time, don't we? We have all known the friend who is dating "that creep" and just can't see him for who he is. It's easy to see in others, but harder to apply to our own lives.

Okay, you may be nodding your head in agreement, and all this makes sense, but you may be asking a very sobering question: What if this "fool" that Proverbs describes is someone close to me, such as a family member? What if the fool that Proverbs is describing is my spouse? Great question. It's a very delicate issue, and one that will be discussed later in this book.

**Principle: Stay away from fools.**

**Life Lesson: Be selective with whom you spend your time, and in whom you place your trust.**

# 10

# DON'T COMMIT ADULTERY

By any reasonable measure, adultery is more common than in past generations, and it is also more accepted by society than it has been in previous generations. Modern culture has different attitudes on monogamy than our parents' generation. Even though most Americans still consider adultery as morally wrong, more of us are engaging in it. It is happening all around us.

Statistics and surveys on rates of infidelity among married couples vary widely. One researcher has reported that there are probably more scientifically worthless "facts" on extramarital relations than on any other facet of human behavior. One of the most prominent surveys on infidelity was conducted by the National Opinion Research Center out of the University of Chicago, which found that about 15–18% of married people have been unfaithful at some point in their marriage.[18] Other research shows the numbers much, much higher. Whatever the real number is, there is a lot of it going on. Even if the number of 15% is accurate, then millions of married men and women in America have been unfaithful to their spouse.

Despite its prevalence in our society, Proverbs is repeatedly clear: Adultery is toxic to your life. Proverbs warns:

Let not your heart turn aside to her ways;
     do not stray into her paths (Prov. 7:25)

For a prostitute is a deep pit;
     an adulteress is a narrow well.
She lies in wait like a robber
     and increases the traitors among mankind.
     (Prov. 23:27-28)

He who commits adultery lacks sense; he who does it
     destroys himself.
He will get wounds and dishonor, and his disgrace will not
     be wiped away.
For jealousy makes a man furious, and he will not spare
     when he takes revenge.
He will accept no compensation; he will refuse though you
     multiply gifts. (Prov 6:32–35)

Okay, I know what you are thinking. Why mention the "adulterous woman" and not the "adulterous man"? Don't worry. Proverbs doesn't let men off the hook either. The connotation here is warning both men and women against the act of engaging in sex with someone other than a spouse. Remember, Solomon wrote Proverbs as an admonition to his son in the context of life under the Mosaic Law. The Mosaic Law strongly prohibited premarital and extramarital sex between men and women, as well as homosexual sex, incest and bestiality.

These verses also refer to the consequences that occur due to illicit affairs, whether they are long-term relationships or one-time encounters. They bring consequences that stay with you for the rest of your life—including the division of your wealth (presumably to support children born of illicit relationships) and enraging a bitter and jealous spouse whose fury cannot be quenched. Either of these consequences is life changing for everyone involved. Four of the most immediately felt consequences of adulterous relationships are as follows:

## *Broken People: The effect on your spouse*

Marriage and family counselor Janice Abrahms Spring has spent over twenty years counseling couples. In *After the Affair*, she describes the emotional devastation involved when a person learns that his or her spouse has been unfaithful. She describes the loss of trust as life altering, with many spouses unable to recover, even to the point of being unable to trust in anyone again. In addition to losing trust, there is a feeling of loss of control—that the hurt spouse has lost control over his or her life. A loss of self-respect is also highly common. The pain and sense of emotional violation, she writes, cuts down to the core of who we are as people. It is common for the offended spouse to feel as if part of them has died. She describes a sense of loss that is unimaginable if it has not been experienced. It can even affect one's will to live.

Losing the ability to trust in others, losing control of your life, losing self-respect, feeling like part of you has died, even affecting one's will to live. Why such a profound impact? Because it is perpetrated by the one and only person capable of causing the most damage. Adultery is the ultimate betrayal, and its impact is compounded by the fact that it was committed by the one person who in uniquely able to hurt you the most. Spring recalls a client's experience in speaking to her husband about his affair,

> When I was fifteen, I was raped. That was nothing compared to your affair. The rapist was a stranger; you, I thought, were my best friend.[19]

A broken spouse is unable to trust and unable make sense of the world around them. It's eminently logical, isn't it? If you wanted to really hurt someone, cause them to doubt their very self worth, render them incapable of functioning in healthy ways, rob them of their ability to enjoy life, and take away the ability to feel, then being unfaithful to them is an effective way to do it.

## *Broken People: The effect on your children*

The impact of an affair upon children is profound. If you are having an affair, there is a very good chance that your children will find out about it. In fact, unbeknownst to you, your children may already know about it. Therapist Emily Brown, in her book *Affairs; A Guide to Working Through the Repercussions of Infidelity*, describes the circumstances of a young man who found out about his father's affair before the betrayed spouse (his mother) found out about the affair.[20] And when this happens, the psychological impact upon them is compounded. In addition to having to deal with the reality that mom or dad is being unfaithful, they are conflicted on whether to say anything about it to the offended spouse. It is a dilemma that they are not equipped to face. They can't adequately process this decision. They often don't say anything because they're afraid that making it known will break up the family, which is their primary reference for, and source of, security. This often brings guilt upon the child for not revealing the secret to the unknowing spouse. These children are in a no-win situation. Keeping silent allows guilt to linger for keeping a parent in the dark. Revealing the secret hurts a spouse and threatens the future of the family. Regardless of whether the child confronts a parent or keeps silent, two things are evident: the child has become an unwilling participant in the saga, and his or her sense of trust has been permanently altered.

Once the affair is brought to light, children usually react in fairly predictable ways. When parents are caught in adultery, children often react with silence. They don't feel safe talking about it, convinced that talking about it may force a decision to break up the family. Some children improperly feel like they are responsible and adopt a false sense of guilt. Many children just can't cope. Unable to process the anger, betrayal, fear and uncertainty, they often respond by acting out in behaviors that were, up to this point taboo and off limits. Their self-destructive behavior is a subconscious cry for help.[21]

Sometimes the emotional damage may not be immediately evident. It can go undetected for years, and it can produce a variety of effects. It can, in some ways, rob them of their childhood. Children whose parents experienced infidelity can have difficulty forming intimate relationships as adults. It can significantly impact their ability to trust others.

Adultery, if it leads to divorce (which happens about 65% of the time), will also impact the children long after the divorce is finalized. Researchers Judith S. Wallerstein, and Sandra Blakeslee have studied the long-term impact of divorce on children. Among their findings:

- One in four children of divorced parents experience a severe and enduring drop in standard of living.

- 60% of children of divorced parents feel rejected by at least one of their parents.

- Almost 50% of children of divorced parents enter adulthood as worried, underachieving, self-deprecating, and sometimes angry young men and women.[22]

Again, if ever there was a way to seriously mess up your kids and impair their ability to form trusting bonds with others, then adultery is one of the most effective means of doing so. If it happens when they are about 12 years old—just entering puberty, that time in their life when rapid changes are taking place in just about every aspect of their lives—then the impact will be felt the hardest. When they find out about the affair (and they probably will) it will be a prime cause of deeply felt pain that will significantly impact their adolescent years, and take decades (and expensive counseling sessions) from which to recover, if they ever do.

## Broken People: The effect on you

As intense as the impact of your affair is on others around you, it will have a profound emotional and psychological impact upon you also. Offending spouses often struggle for years to forgive themselves for the hurt and pain that they cause. And some offending spouses are never able to forgive themselves. You may, in all likelihood, need the help of qualified professionals to effectively deal with the guilt. Forgiving yourself is not easy. It's not as simple as acknowledging the mistake and moving on. Guilt and shame impact our lives in profound ways. It is not uncommon for an offending spouse to act out in self-destructive behavior as a form of self-punishment. One of the most destructive aspects of guilt is that it keeps us from moving forward in a healthy way.

## Destroyed Marriages

There is probably nothing that can destroy a marriage faster than marital infidelity. The University of Chicago survey, mentioned earlier, found that only about 35% of marriages survive an affair.

## Financial Consequences

If the adultery leads to divorce it often will result in two mortgages (or two rents) two water bills, two heating bills, two cable bills, etc. Ouch! It hurts even to contemplate, doesn't it? And women are hit the hardest. About twenty-one percent of newly divorced women live below the poverty line, compared to only nine percent of newly divorced men. Natalie Nelson, a financial divorce consultant in Boulder, Colorado, says, "I wonder sometimes if people knew what divorce was going to cost them if they would try at all costs to avoid that outcome."[23]

Broken people, guilt, shame, destroyed marriages, and financial ruin. Pretty sobering, isn't it? It is no wonder that Proverbs is strongly emphatic on the issue of adultery.

Don't commit adultery. As obvious as the admonition is on its face, you would be surprised at the number of people, even self-professed, Bible-believing Christians who will go to extremes and engage in intellectual gymnastics to justify their adulterous relationships. Janis Spring lists some of the most common justifications that people use to excuse or rationalize their affair:

- My affair is ok as long as I love the other person.

- My affair is ok as long as I don't love the other person.

- My affair is ok as long as my spouse doesn't find out.

- What my spouse doesn't know won't hurt them.

- A one night stand/fling doesn't change our relationship.

- I only have one life to lead and I deserve to be as happy as possible. Its ok to get some of my needs met from my lover and the rest from my spouse.

- My affair has made me a happier person and therefore I am a happier spouse.

- My affair allows me to satisfy my needs without breaking up the family... I'm doing it for the kids.

- People aren't meant to be monogamous.

- My biological instinct is to be adulterous.

- I have no impulse control.

- All men are wolves.

- Every couple has its secrets.

- I'm entitled to keep part of myself hidden and separate from my spouse.

- Since my spouse probably knows about my affair, but isn't confronting me, it must be okay, as long as I don't flaunt it.

- I shouldn't have to sacrifice what I need in order to make my partner feel secure or happy.

- I never promised to be perfect.

- If I commit myself fully to any one person, I'm bound to get hurt.[24]

Do you see the twisted logic used in some of these justifications? We've already acknowledged that adultery is happening all around us. The perception of greener pastures is a prominent and common idea that appeals when life gets hard. How can we deal with the temptations of modern society, where anonymous sexual encounters and illicit relationships are promised just a mouse click away?

I believe that in this case, an ounce of prevention is truly worth a pound of cure. It's much easier to prevent adultery than to recover from it. There are scores of helpful tools to help you protect your marriage from adultery. Most of them incorporate and build upon these basic ideas:

1. A commitment to purity in the relationship

2. Maintaining good communication with your spouse

3. A willingness to be teachable and correctible

4. Setting parameters: knowing your own weaknesses and being accountable to others for your weaknesses

It's vitally important to remember that there is the possibility of hope and restoration after infidelity. A broken marriage can be restored. Connie Neal, whose husband Patrick confessed to her that he had committed adultery, describes the heartache she faced because of her husband's infidelity.

"His revelation was as unbelievable as if someone had told me the moon had fallen from the sky," Connie recalled: "The man who told me he'd lived a secret life of sexual sin seemed so different from the man to whom I'd been married for nine years."[25]

Naturally, in the initial days and weeks after Patrick's confession, her rage, disillusionment, and confusion were intense.

"Yet," Connie says, "Pat was so broken, so willing to do whatever it took to break free from his sexual addiction, that despite my anger and hurt, I agreed to go through counseling with him. There came a moment during counseling when I thought our marriage would end.... It was only my confidence in God that gave me the courage to hold on."

> There is the possibility of hope and restoration after infidelity. A broken marriage can be restored.

Over the following months, Pat did change. With help, he overcame his sexual addictions and became a better husband. As a wife, Connie grew as well. As the months turned into years, Pat and Connie one day realized that God had healed and restored their marriage. Rejecting anger and bitterness, Connie says: "I had to choose—with God's help—to remember that if God could forgive Pat's wrongs, I could, too. Today, several years after Pat's confession, thanks to God's love and power, our life together is better than ever before."[26]

Recovering from adultery is a process. Underlying issues that lead to adultery take time and effort to address. But, if infidelity and adultery is affecting your marriage right now, there is hope.

**Principle: Don't commit adultery.**

**Life Lesson: Take the necessary steps to protect your marriage and your sexual purity.**

# 11

# DISCIPLINE YOUR CHILDREN

Children are at once the most rewarding experience and the most demanding challenge that life offers. No job is harder and more challenging, no responsibility is greater, and no task is more rewarding. Proverbs has much to say about raising children:

> He who spares the rod hates his son, but he who loves him
>     is careful to discipline him. (13:24)

> Discipline your son, for there is hope. (Prov. 19:18a)

> Folly is bound up in the heart of a child,
>     but the rod of discipline drives it far from him.
>     (Prov. 22:15)

> Do not withhold discipline from a child;
>     if you strike him with a rod, he will not die.
>     (Prov. 23:13)

> But a child left to himself brings shame to his mother.
>     (Prov. 29:15b)

Discipline your son, and he will give you rest. (Prov. 29:17a)

I am not going to expound on what form of discipline parents should use. The connotation is discipline, but Proverbs' charge to discipline children is deeper. This charge is speaking about the greater responsibility of raising a child, of which discipline is an indispensable aspect. Discipline is not just correcting them. Discipline involves the larger responsibility to instill character. The parental responsibility to discipline children is a sacred responsibility.

> The parental responsibility to discipline children is a sacred responsibility.

Children are not naturally wise. They are naturally drawn to foolishness. If not taught the difference between the two, they will gravitate toward foolishness. This must be recognized and understood. Discipline is all about the commitment on the part of the parents to instill character. To be willing to discipline a child requires investing your time and your energy. It is hard work. It is inconvenient. It interrupts your busy schedule. It requires maturity on your part. It stretches you. It is one of the most important ways that you show love for your children. If you neglect disciplining your children, you are not loving them. You are hurting them.

Brenda lived in our neighborhood some time ago. We (and the rest of our neighbors) noticed that Brenda did not discipline her daughter. She did not correct her 6-year-old daughter—ever. She actually avoided correcting her daughter. She allowed the child to speak harshly to her, and to talk down to her. The daughter treated her mother like the mother was the servant. The little girl literally ordered her mother around and even threatened her. It was the most remarkable dynamic I had ever seen between a parent and child. There was no discipline to be seen. It was actually quite uncomfortable to hear and made for some odd interactions.

To be present when the child threw one of her many tantrums was uncomfortable to say the least. I saw Proverbs 29:15 first hand. The child's poor behavior was more a vivid reflection on Brenda's poor parenting than it was on the daughter. The kid was just doing what kids will do.

One day I pointed out that I couldn't help but notice that the way that the daughter spoke to Brenda was highly unusual. Brenda intimated that her parents had been overbearing and overly authoritative. Brenda's treatment of her daughter was a reaction (and a very unhealthy overreaction) to how Brenda's father had treated her as a child. Brenda thought that by letting her child have anything she wanted, she was loving her. But the truth was just the opposite. By not disciplining her child, Brenda was hurting her and making herself look bad.

Noted pediatrician and author Dr. T. Berry Brazelton warns:

"A child who has not been disciplined to learn self-control by the time he is old enough to be unsupervised by parents... is a child in danger."[27]

Proverbs teaches that if you love your children you will take the time and effort to correct them and teach them the values they need for life. Disciplining children is inconvenient. It takes great patience. In fact, it is some of the hardest work you'll ever do. No one will pay you for it, nor may anyone ever recognize your efforts. As noted author and psychologist Dr. James Dobson has written, parenting isn't for cowards. Neither is parenting for the lazy or for the faint of heart.

> "A child who has not been disciplined to learn self-control by the time he is old enough to be unsupervised by parents... is a child in danger."

Disciplining your children requires that you learn from others. No one is a natural born parent. You may have maternal or paternal instincts, but you must learn how to properly raise kids. You can do great harm to your children out of well-intentioned ignorance. Children truly are the product of their environment, and parents can do more harm to their children than anyone else.

The underlying principle of Proverbs' admonitions on discipline is that your children are your responsibility, given to you by God. It is a sacred trust. Be a good steward of that responsibility. Make the raising of your children a primary life goal. Do not neglect it. The world is full of selfish parents that don't make the effort. It's full of busy people that don't make it a priority, who allow other responsibilities to crowd out the very thing that must be a priority. Don't neglect it.

Robert Lewis is a pastor in Little Rock, Arkansas. On the morning of his daughter Elizabeth's wedding, she asked her mom and dad if she could read them a letter. Here is that letter:

> "Dear Mom and Dad, I am overwhelmed at the enormous task of recapping and thanking you for what you have taught, modeled and sacrificed for me over the past 27 years. The blessings you have poured out over the decades have been unbelievable, and I am only now realizing the magnitude of all you were to me. I am here today, this day, happier than I have ever been, marrying the most wonderful man, because of you—your prayers—your gentle push to trusting and following the Lord, your sacrifice, your quiet guidance on consequences good and bad, for the direction my life would take because of the decisions I was up against. Dad, I know what a real man is because of you—a man after God's own heart, a leader, a provider, a lover to your wife and father to your children. I knew what kind of man I wanted to marry because of you. You and I are

kindred spirits, and I don't know what I would have done without our long talks.

Thank you for taking me to swim practice at 4:30 in the morning.

Thank you for walking with me on the Great Wall of China when I was 11 years old, and giving me a love for travel.

Thank you for always encouraging me to dream big.

For hosting the best birthday parties ever.

For always making me feel special.

For letting Katie and me go backpacking in Europe when we were only 18.

For encouraging me to go [to] graduate school.

For being proud of me and telling me you were.

For letting me make mistakes.

For never missing a swim meet, or basketball or volleyball game.

For showing me what a good marriage is supposed to look like.

For bringing us back presents when you went to speak out of town.

For making a big deal out of little accomplishments.

For teaching me about being good with money.

For giving me Mom's Camry…. just because.

For taking us to Colorado in the summer.

For spending time with me on dates or shopping trips – even with three kids in the family.

For the best Christmases every year.

For praising me in front of your friends.

For teaching me the value of hard work.

For praying for me.

For teaching me that details count.

For taking us out to eat or to party when we experience little accomplishments and victories.

For reading us the *Chronicles of Narnia*.

For being on my side when life and people seemed to be against me.

For all those two and three line emails pointing me to trust in God.

For always loving me, no matter what.

On this day, I am so honored to be known as Robert Lewis' daughter."[28]

That morning at the breakfast table, Robert Lewis cried upon hearing those words. He describes that instance as one of the greatest moments of his life. What a legacy Robert Lewis has left to his daughter Elizabeth. And to her children also.

What greater achievement can one accomplish than to launch a life into the future? It requires effort. Did Elizabeth Lewis become a grateful, thankful, well-adjusted, responsible adult by accident? By default? No. She is the woman she is largely because her father and mother took the time to nurture and train her.

**Principle: Discipline your children.**

**Life Lesson: Make the discipline of your children a priority.**

# 12

# LEARN TO CONTROL YOUR TEMPER

Proverbs repeatedly warns of the problems created by a hot temper.

Whoever is slow to anger has great understanding,
but he who has a hasty temper exalts folly.
(Prov. 14:29)

A soft answer turns away wrath,
But a harsh word stirs up anger. (Prov. 15:1)

A hot-tempered man stirs up strife,
but he who is slow to anger quiets contention.
(Prov. 15:18)

Whoever is slow to anger is better than the mighty,
and he who rules his spirit than he who takes a city.
(Prov. 16:32)

Good sense makes one slow to anger. (Prov. 19:11a)

A man without self-control is like a city broken into and left
without walls. (Prov. 25:28)

Make no friendship with a man given to anger,
nor go with a wrathful man, lest you learn his ways and
    entangle yourself in a snare. (Prov. 22:24-25)

A fool gives full vent to his spirit,
but a wise man quietly holds it back. (Prov. 29:11)

We see from Proverbs 14:29 that losing your temper makes
a fool out of you. Losing your temper highlights your folly. It
reflects badly upon you. How many times have you seen this in
public? Someone loses their temper and creates a scene. A few
years ago my wife and I were on a double date with some dear
friends in Old Town Alexandria, Virginia, walking near the
waterfront boardwalk near the Potomac River, when we saw a
father lose his temper with his daughter. From what we could
ascertain, she had arranged to meet a boy down on the boardwalk
and had not told her father. As we were walking, we saw the father
walk up behind the girl, snatch the cell phone out of her hand, and
throw it into the Potomac River as far and as hard as he could,
while yelling at the top of his lungs how much he did not appreciate his daughter's dishonesty in arranging to meet the boy. Then
the yelling started between the father and the daughter, who was
justifiably upset that her father had just launched her phone into
the river. It was ugly. Needless to say, everyone witnessing the
outburst felt extremely uncomfortable. The daughter was embarrassed beyond words, and all of the bystanders were embarrassed
for her.

The daughter's actions were not to be excused, but the way
that the father handled the situation was a disaster. Rather than
rationally confronting the pair in a calm tone, the father turned
a bad situation into something much worse by losing his temper. There is no doubt in my mind that that event will be forever
etched in the daughter's memory, a defining moment in her relationship with the man that obviously cares a great deal about her,
but has trouble finding ways to express his fatherly concern.

This issue of temper and anger is no small deal. The father's actions were like an arsonist setting a field aflame with one spark. A quick-tempered person can quickly turn a normal situation into a bad one—and a bad situation into a disaster.

Alec Baldwin is well known as one of the four Baldwin brothers that make their living as actors. Alec is also known for his premier starring roles in popular Hollywood feature films like *The Hunt for Red October, The Ghosts of Mississippi,* and *Pearl Harbor.* But in April 2007, Baldwin became known publicly for something that shocked his fans around the world.

The Internet site, TMZ, released a recorded phone conversation in which Baldwin had left a scathing phone voicemail message and tirade directed toward his 11-year-old daughter, Ireland. Apparently, his young daughter (aka Addie) had failed to answer his pre-arranged phone call to her. At the time, Baldwin was locked in a bitter three-year custody battle with his ex-wife, actress Kim Basinger, whom he had divorced in 2006. Baldwin's loss of temper and angry, hurtful, threatening words directed at his young daughter, startled listeners.[29]

Baldwin's brutal tone of voice lit up the entertainment wire for well over a week. Millions of people that didn't have a strong opinion of Baldwin now saw him as a monster. Although Baldwin issued a public apology to his daughter and to his fans, the damage to both his daughter and to his reputation had been done. It was truly humiliating for both of them.

But Alec Baldwin is no monster. He is nice guy, who, at times, is quite charming. I met him several years before this episode and was struck by his quick wit and intelligence. The point is that this event could happen to anyone. The potential for anger is there in each and every one of us all the time. Emotions are quickly ignited...joy, sadness, fear, anger. Words and actions of others quickly stir these emotions. A quick temper is simply the lack of self-control over the emotions that are already there, simmering or smoldering just below the surface. Proverbs says that when a quick-tempered man (person) stirs up strife and anger (15:1;

15:18), he literally fans the flame in others. Anger is contagious because it provokes others to respond in a like manner. Anger is like stoking coals. If you leave them alone they'll eventually go out, but if you stoke them or stir them, they flame up.

This is why Proverbs warns against even hanging around with violent tempered people.

> Make no friendship with a man given to anger, nor go with a wrathful man, lest you learn his ways and entangle yourself in a snare. (Prov. 22:24-25)

Proverbs repeatedly refers to a hot-tempered man as a fool (Prov 29:11). Anger, or lacking self-control, is a very real problem that can ruin your life. This is a truth that a good friend of mine found out a few years ago. Lonnie was a great guy with a real servant's heart, and he could be a very tender person. He was a very hard worker. He was tall, muscular, very masculine and extremely handsome. He was a faithful friend that always had my back. I remember thinking many times that if I were ever in a foxhole, the one guy I would want with me would be Lonnie; tough as nails, loyal and a man of true conviction. But he had a secret that no one knew of and that he didn't reveal to anyone. It didn't become public until just a few years ago. Lonnie couldn't control his temper, and for years he physically abused his wife. It went on for years, unknown to anyone, until his children became big enough to defend their mother. A few years ago, the familiar sequence of events ensued, he became angry and began lashing out, only this time his grown son stepped up in defense of those not big enough to hit back—and the dam burst. This time it couldn't be swept under the rug. Now there was someone just as big hitting back, so the police were involved. Now charges were filed. Now it became public.

The words of Proverbs 25:28 ring true in this situation. The verse describes a city broken into and without walls. It is a picture of a village that has been ransacked. All that has been achieved—food supply, homes, possessions, family members, all of the people and physical possessions that one treasures in this life—has been ravaged, brutally violated, destroyed, or stolen. It was carried off by a ruthless enemy that had no concern for life or property. Lonnie's lack of control over his temper rendered his life like this village. His marriage was in ruins. His career and his reputation were damaged, and his relationship with his children was forever marred. All that he had worked for had forever changed. Today Lonnie's wife is remarried, and Lonnie has remarried as well. I pray that he is receiving the help and restoration he needs.

How can you learn to control your anger? Proverbs 19:11 says discretion is the key to controlling anger. "A man's discretion makes him slow to anger." Discretion is a choice. Proverbs instructs us to choose to control our anger. Recognizing the problem (and being willing to do something about it) is half the battle. Once we acknowledge the problem, we can choose to control our anger. A quick temper is an impulsive reaction that shows a lack of self-control. Controlling our temper is a choice. It is a skill one can learn. It takes practice and discipline, but it can be done. And it must be done.

> Wisdom acts intentionally to address the problem before it's too late.

As we will see in later chapters, a fundamental tool for this and other issues is placing yourself in relationship with others that can help you identify why you are getting angry, how to process your emotions and help you develop the skills to respond appropriately, and become accountable when you fail. The wise thing to do is to take action. Wisdom acts intentionally to address the problem before it's too late. Wisdom calls those with anger issues to get the help they need today—to place themselves in a nurturing community that can equip them with the tools they need to work through their anger.

Time and experience help here. The hard knocks of life can teach valuable lessons in this area. People do pick up wisdom as they age. This is why some people seem to mellow with age, and learn through the years to have greater control over their tempers. Many people have seen first-hand the destruction they, or someone near them, has caused through a lack of self-control. They look back in regret over a life of broken friendships, inflamed arguments that could have been avoided if they, or someone near them, had used more discretion.

But you don't have to learn the hard way. Choose now to get control over your temper.

**Principle: Learn to control your temper.**

**Life Lesson: If you have a bad temper, make it an immediate priority to seek help and adopt the skills needed to manage your anger.**

# 13

# RESPECT THE OPINIONS OF OTHERS

The one who states his case first seems right,
until the other comes and examines him.
(Prov. 18:17)

The obvious admonition, on its face here, is that it is unwise to rush to judgment. One person sounds right until another comes and presents his case. When opposing views are weighed against each other, the comparison points out the strengths, as well as the limitations and inadequacies, of each opinion. What first appears reasonable can change once more data and opinions are brought to bear on the situation at hand.

But the deeper lesson in this proverb is that your first impression may be inadequate or even inaccurate. One key aspect of this principle should be applied when we encounter a person with whom we disagree. When we encounter someone who expresses his or her opinion, or strongly held attitudes that we disagree with (or that may sound downright ridiculous, or even offensive), our first reaction is often to reject it outright. The immediate reaction is to show our disapproval.

Often we may roll our eyes or scoff. At a minimum we mentally discount what we are hearing. But reacting to such a person immediately, particularly with emotion, is very, very unwise. It's wise to apply the idea expressed in this proverb: *don't rush to judgment.* But it's also wise to apply the underlying principle: *Don't immediately discount the opinion of others, regardless of how much you may disagree with their point of view.*

Patient listening, without reacting with emotion, is a very valuable life skill. It is an invaluable conflict resolution skill that will pay huge dividends for you in many areas of your life. Conflict resolution skills are among the most valuable skills one can develop. If you can effectively resolve conflicts,

> Don't immediately discount the opinion of others, regardless of how much you may disagree with their point of view.

you can save yourself a lot of grief. Moreover, it can help you stand out among your peers. When you listen patiently, even to people with whom you vehemently disagree, you appear to others as uncommonly reasonable, patient, confident, wise, mature, and strong. Responding too quickly, much like responding in anger, fuels the fire of emotions. Listening patiently to the opinions of others shows respect for them.

Patient listening may reveal that sometimes our first reaction would have been inappropriate, and that the other person's opinion is not that outlandish. Sometimes we will discover that they were actually correct in their initial opinion or observation. When this happens, we end up learning something new.

You will always have disagreements with the opinions of some people. It is easy to discount the opinions of those with whom we disagree. But remember, there is always a reason for the opinions and attitudes that people hold. There is always a reason people do the things they do. Even if you don't agree with them, learn to listen to what they have to say before you respond. Often, you will hear the reason *behind* the opinion, and you will become wiser.

**Principle: Respect the opinions of others.**

**Life Lesson: Learn to withhold immediate reaction to other peoples' opinions.**

# 14

# LIVE IN COMMUNITY

Whoever isolates himself seeks his own desire;
  he breaks out against all sound judgment.
  (Prov. 18:1)

The Hebrew word for isolate, or "separate," used here, is *parad* (paw-rad), which means *to break, spread, separate, disperse or divide, to place out of joint, to scatter abroad, to sever one's self.* To separate one's self from others is to quarrel with all sound wisdom. How is separating yourself from others quarrelling with wisdom? Because to separate oneself from others is to directly negate the only method of obtaining wisdom. Wisdom only comes from being in community with others.

We are not islands. We need other people. You need other people. The principle of living in community is similar to the principle of listening discussed in Chapter 3, but it is even more basic and fundamental. Yes, you need other people to help you and encourage you. But, you also need other people to challenge you. You need other people to *inconvenience* you.

You were designed to enjoy the results of a healthy and robust community. But you can enjoy these benefits only if you do the hard work of getting along with others. If you can't get along with others, you won't enjoy the benefits that community brings.

> You need other people to inconvenience you.

This is a critical part of the larger design for your life. God placed you in a family for you to be nurtured, but He also designed your family as the laboratory for you to learn the basic life skills needed to properly function—life skills like patience, humility, courtesy, and conflict resolution. You either learn these skills, or you become isolated and cut off from the community. Community is God's laboratory. It is His way of using others as the sandpaper in our lives. If you are cut off from others, your opportunity for progress seriously diminishes, because only in community will you be able to have the rough edges rubbed off. Only in community will you learn to get along with others and become the kind of person that is likeable. God places us in community with others for the purpose of developing these critical life skills.

Getting along with others is hard to do. It is not often our preferred response, and it is not convenient. This is the general idea conveyed in Proverbs 18:1. But I believe a more specific message is being conveyed: the necessity of accountability and advice, and the importance of being surrounded by those willing to tell you what you need to hear, not just what you want to hear.

I've seen this principle demonstrated many times in my life and in the lives of those I love. That is why I'm a big believer in the power of third party assistance. Marriage counseling, for example, is a powerful, wonderful, and often misunderstood, tool that is under-utilized. If couples are humble, willing and able to submit their key marriage issues to a well-qualified, third party—a neutral observer who doesn't have an agenda other than the couple's personal benefit—it is amazing what can occur. Most of the successful marriages I know of have used a marriage counselor or a marriage coach. Seeing a marriage counselor is not an admission of failure, but an admission of a desire for help. There isn't a marriage that doesn't have very real and complicated issues that threaten its vitality. Having a marriage coach to help couples work through these issues is invaluable. This concept of marriage counseling or a marriage coach is, on a mini-scale, the practical application of the principle of living in community.

Living in community can take different forms. We've discussed two of them. One of the more popular forms is a prayer group, or accountability group. I and many others I know, have participated in such a group. I participated with three other men in such a group for about eight years. We originally came together because we realized that we needed a greater degree of accountability in our lives. We realized that our desire to be faithful husbands and fathers, as noble as it is, was threatened by the barrage of pressures and temptations that modern life brings. So we began meeting regularly to share our challenges and to pray for one another. It has never been a formal thing – just an open, honest and consistent dialogue about our frustrations, our challenges, our hopes and our dreams. It usually involves prayer and an opportunity to ask questions of each other that reveal our deeper issues and cut through the fluff. Here is just a sampling of some of these questions:

- What are you hoping for?

- What areas are you struggling with?

- During your upcoming business trip, where are you tempted to go during your down time? During your recent business trip, did you go there?

- Have you visited inappropriate sites on the Internet?

- Have you spoken in an inappropriate way to a female in the last two weeks?

- What steps can you take to minimize that temptation and its effect on you?

- Are there areas of your finances that won't stand up under scrutiny if you were audited or if it were splashed on the front page of the newspaper?

- How have you honored your wife in the last week?

- How are you applying your gifts and your talents?

- What are you doing to continue growing spiritually?

- What are you doing to move toward the goals you have set for your life?

- When was the last time you spoke to your wife or children inappropriately?

- Have you just lied to me?

As you can see, these questions get right to the core. Being in this environment forces a person to deal with issues that most of us seldom examine on our own. My own experience with my group forced me to look at some hard and often unpleasant things about my habits and my personality. It has literally forced me to change my attitudes and my behavior. These close friends are literally the only guys in the world that can look me in the eye and say, "You are being a jerk on that issue," or "You are wrong in this issue," or "Stop being so stubborn." They can get away with this because I know they have my best interests at heart. They love me unconditionally. They have no agenda other than that they are for me and for my success. They know me and love me anyway, in spite of my many weaknesses and vices.

This is community. And it has yielded benefits that I had not anticipated when we began meeting together years ago. One of the benefits of this group is that it has bonded me with these men. We are going to be friends for life. We have a degree of relationship that is rare. It is a community of men that I value as among the most important things in my life. I am a better man because of these men and the investment they have made in my life.

John Eldredge, in his book *Waking the Dead*, describes the difficulty in forming this type of community.

> A true community is something you will have to fight for. You'll have to fight to get one, and you'll have to fight to keep it afloat. But you fight for it like you bail out a life raft during a storm at sea. You want this thing to work. You need this thing to work. You can't ditch it and jump back on the cruise ship. This is the church; this is all you have. Without it, you'll go down. Or back to prison. Suddenly all those "one another's" in Scripture make sense. Love one another. Bear one another's burdens. Forgive one another. Acts of kindness become deeply meaningful because we know we are at war. Knowing full well that we are all facing battles of our own, we give one another the benefit of the doubt. *Leigh isn't intentionally being distant from me—she's probably under an assault.* That's why you must know each other's stories, know how to "read" one another. A word of encouragement can heal a wound; a choice to forgive can destroy a stronghold. You never knew your simple acts were so weighty. It's what we've come to call "lifestyle warfare." We check in regularly with one another, not out of paranoia ("Do you still like me?"), but in order to watch over each other's hearts."[30]

Your community will take a variety of forms; a small group or Bible study, a reading/discussion group that covers a book you've found meaningful, or a consistent time with friends to bike, hike, run, bowl or any number of other past-times. It could be just a one-on-one consistent time with someone you trust over coffee. Whatever works for you, the important point is to open up and live in community. You were designed for it. If you will do this, you will find a greater appreciation for other people. You will become a better person. And you will become wiser.

**Principle: Live in community.**

**Life Lesson: Purposefully place yourself in close relationships with others.**

# PART IV

# PERSONAL MANAGEMENT, BUSINESS & FINANCE

# 15

## LIVE ON A BUDGET

Know well the condition of your flocks, and give attention
   to your herds,
for riches do not last forever; and does a crown endure
   to all generations? (Prov. 27:23-24)

In ancient times, land and animals were two of the most
common and valuable commodities. One's wealth was often
measured in terms of the size of one's flocks of cattle, sheep
or goats. To the modern reader, the above admonition sounds
bizarre or even silly, but to one with even a cursory understanding of life in Biblical times, the instruction is clear: maintain a
precise understanding of your current financial situation. Know
accurately how your incoming cash flow compares against your
expenses. In modern vernacular, this means develop a budget.

No one would dare launch a business without a business plan.
No bank will loan you money without seeing the basic elements
of a business plan, the essential components of which include
one's expected revenues and expenses. Yet, 60% of Americans
don't have a personal budget. That's right, only 40% of Americans
have a personal household budget.[31]

This figure just floors me. It is truly amazing in today's world. No wonder so many people find themselves upside down with debt. A budget is an absolutely indispensable tool for personal money management.

Not having a budget can lead to unneeded stress. Any marriage and family therapist will tell you that money problems are one of the most common reasons for conflict in marriage. This is especially concerning because the money problem is a problem that can be solved. If money issues are straining your marriage, move intentionally to fix them. There are many resources to help you develop a budget and stick to it. Two widely used resources are Crown Financial Ministries out of Knoxville, Tennessee and Financial Peace University, which is operated by talk radio host Dave Ramsey out of Nashville, Tennessee. Both ministries offer excellent resources to help you establish and stick to a personal budget. Their resources include suggested categories to include in your budget along with suggested percentages of your income that should be spent for each category. These can be found at www.crown.org and www.daveramsey.com.

Those seeking to live wisely should develop a budget and stick to it.

**Principle: Live on a budget.**

**Life Lesson: Develop a personal household budget and stick to it.**

# 16

# PERSISTENT HARD WORK WILL PAY OFF

D iligence is defined in the dictionary as "Constant and earnest effort to accomplish what is undertaken; persistent exertion of body or mind."

The emphasis is the persistent application of hard work *over time* (Dictionary.com).

Proverbs teaches us the importance of this:

A slack hand causes poverty,
    but the hand of the diligent makes rich. (Prov. 10:4)

The hand of the diligent will rule,
    while the slothful will be put to forced labor.
    (Prov. 12:24)

The precious possession of a man is diligence.
    (12:27 NASB95)

While the soul of the diligent is richly supplied.
    (Prov. 13:4b)

The plans of the diligent lead surely to abundance.
(Prov. 21:5a)

The Hebrew word for diligence is *charutz*, which means to incise or cut as if to dig a trench or as if to mine for gold. (The word is taken from a root word *charatz* which means to cut sharply as if to wound.) The implication of *charutz* is not just to cut or dig once but to keep digging and digging and digging as if to plow a trench, or keep digging as if digging for gold. The emphasis is on the pattern of repetition that is ongoing over time.

Diligence cannot be demonstrated in an instant or a day or a week. Diligence can only be demonstrated through an ongoing, continual, consistent effort. It is a sustaining effort that continues over a period of several weeks, months and even years.

There are two inherent benefits gained from diligence as it pertains to business. The first is what I refer to as *experience over time*. As you work diligently (working hard over a sustained period of time) your skills, experience, and expertise increase. And as these increase, your responsibilities will increase. Why? Because your skills have rendered you inherently valuable. Your experience and skills enable you to offer something of intrinsic value to the marketplace that people will pay for. They inherently make you stand out from your peers. You have something unique that very few can provide. As a result, your influence increases and your ability to earn builds. The natural inertia is toward promotion and higher wages, and the longer you continue working diligently, the more value you build. In many cases your wages and influence don't just increase, they multiply.

How many senior managers started out as entry-level employees? How many sales managers started out at the bottom in entry-level sales? Almost all of them. You see it over and over: the diligent salesperson is made a manager over several territories, then over a region. He or she becomes responsible for an area that is much larger, sometimes exponentially larger than their former area. Once responsible for a part of a city, he or she next manages several states and eventually they become the national sales manager. They might even move into corporate management and run part of the company. It's a familiar pattern. Start out as a salesman, manage a group of sales staff, then manage a team of managers, and in time, earn a multiple of the original salary.

This principle applies collectively to companies also. One example is the R. W. Beckett Corporation outside of Cleveland that manufactures residential and commercial oil burners. John Beckett took over what was a small family business in the 1960s and over the years grew the company's revenues a hundredfold. Today Beckett Corporation is a global leader in its field. The company's growth is due primarily to John Beckett's diligence. He describes his responsibility as CEO as a stewardship, and he explains that his diligent work ethic is because he wants to provide a livelihood for hundreds of employees that are like family.

The second inherent benefit gained from diligence in business is the *raw power of wealth accumulation over time.* One of the most basic rules of money and finance that is essential for everyone to understand is the power of compound interest. And one of the basic principles everyone should know regarding compound interest is called "the rule of 72." The rule of 72 is a tool to determine how long it will take you to double your money in a passive account (when you are not putting in any additional funds). Simply divide 72 by the interest rate that you are receiving. A passive account drawing 8% interest doubles in nine years ($72/8 = 9$). A 12% savings or return on your money doubles in six years. 18% interest doubles your savings in four years ($72/18 = 4$). So $1,000 earning 18% interest will double in four years.

This is a good yield for a passive investment (a one-time investment with no additional funds added), but let's look at what happens if you keep adding to your investment. Rather than a one time investment of $1,000, let's add 1$ per day to it. So start with $1,000 and add $365 per year. You'll see that small savings, set aside regularly (diligently) over time, will grow exponentially.

The chart below shows what happens. (This chart shows the power of tax-free compound interest, which you can get in a retirement vehicle such as an IRA). As you can see, the power of compound interest is truly astounding. $1,000 increased by $365 per year, invested at different interest rates yields the following:

| Interest Rate | 6% | 8% | 12% |
|---|---|---|---|
| Year 1 | $1,447 | $1,474 | $1,529 |
| Year 3 | $2,422 | $2,539 | $2,784 |
| Year 5 | $3,519 | $3,781 | $4,359 |
| Year 7 | $4,751 | $5,231 | $6,335 |
| Year 9 | $6,135 | $6,921 | $8,813 |
| Year 11 | $7,690 | $8,893 | $11,922 |
| Year 45 | $96,075 | $184,281 | $719,232 |

One dollar per day invested (at 12% interest rate) over the course of a lifetime of work, from the age of 20 to 65, will yield $719,000. Notice the enormous difference as a result of the interest rate.

Now consider this: If you have the commitment and diligence to invest $1 per day when you are 20, you will probably have the same diligence, and increased earning power to be able to invest $3 per day by the time you are 30. If you can afford $3 per day when you are 30, then you should be able to invest 5$ per day by the time you are 40. What would your retirement account look like then?

Invest $1 per day from age 20 to 30, and then $3 per day from age 30 to 40, and then $5 per day from age 40-65. If you did, then by the time you are 30, you'd have $10,280 By the time you were 40 you'd have $53,450. By the time you are 65, you'd have $1.181 million. That is the power of diligent work over time. No get rich quick formula. No special tricks. Just diligent work and diligent savings.

There is another aspect regarding diligence in saving—and you can see it in the example above: the element of time. And specifically the value of starting early. Starting early is crucial, and if you will start early the payout is staggering.

Here is an example: John's IRA earns 12% per year. He saves $2,000 per year for six years. Then he never puts another dollar into his IRA. His total investment is $12,000.

Meanwhile, Sean does not save during these same six years. But after these six years, Sean starts investing $2,000 per year until he retires. Sean earns the same 12% interest per year that John earns. But Sean's investment is $74,000.

The chart below shows the value of John and Sean's respective IRAs, from the time they are 22 years old throughout their career until they retire at age 65. Remember, John's total investment is $12,000 ($2,000 per year for the first six years), while Sean's is $74,000 ($2,000 per year for the last 37 years).

| Age | John: $12k inv. | Sean: $74k inv. |
|-----|-----------------|-----------------|
| 22 | $2,240 | $0 |
| 23 | 4,509 | 0 |
| 24 | 7,050 | 0 |
| 25 | 9,896 | 0 |
| 26 | 13,083 | 0 |
| 27 | 16,653 | 0 |
| 28 | 18,652 | 2,240 |
| 29 | 20,890 | 4,509 |
| 30 | 23,397 | 7,050 |
| 35 | 41,233 | 25,130 |
| 40 | 72,667 | 56,993 |
| 45 | 128,064 | 113,147 |
| 50 | 225,692 | 212,598 |
| 55 | 397,746 | 386,516 |
| 60 | 700,965 | 693,879 |
| 65 | 1,235,339 | 1,235,557 |

With compound interest, the earlier you start saving, the greater the accumulated interest on your original investment. The important thing is to *start* saving your money now. The best time to start saving is now—no matter how large or small the amount. It's never too early—or late—to start. Remember, today is the first day of the rest of your life, so get time on your side and plan for your future by starting to save NOW.

Most of my close friends are middle-aged and they understand this principle of saving. They get it—not because they did it, or because they woke up one day and discovered it—but because they regret not having executed this strategy much earlier in life.

It doesn't just work with IRAs or tax-exempt vehicles, but savings and investing in general. If you (or your parents) would have bought a few shares of IBM in the 60's or a few shares of Wal-Mart in the early 80's or Microsoft, Amazon.com or Google when they went public and held on to them through their stock divisions, your financial situation would probably look different than it does today. Picking winners and losers in the stock market is a risk, and you'll probably miss more than you hit. But the good news is that you don't have to pick stocks. You can have the same effect by just getting started early in safe investment vehicles.

If these ideas are new to you, I hope that you are beginning to see that it's not necessarily how much you earn that will determine whether you end up "rich" and successful, as much as it is a matter of 1) working diligently over time, 2) saving diligently over time, and 3) getting started early. Proverbs confirms this strategy in chapter 13:

> Wealth gained hastily will dwindle,
>     but whoever gathers little by little will increase it.
>     (Prov. 13:11)

Hard work over a long period of time, along with being diligent to earn and diligent to save are the keys. Diligent work and diligent savings will provide for you and your family. It's a solid recipe for financial security for the long term. These two powerful factors, experience over time and the raw power of wealth accumulation over time, will work for you if you are diligent.

One other aspect to diligence must be mentioned: Diligence is also an attitude about the nature of work and the nature of money. In his best-selling book *Rich Dad, Poor Dad*, Robert Kiyosaki describes the two men in his life (his birth father and his stepfather) that influenced his thinking regarding work and money. His "poor dad" was actually his birth father. He was highly educated, had a Ph.D. from the finest universities in the country, and enjoyed a substantial income. Yet, in spite of a successful teaching career, he struggled financially all of his life. When he died, all he was able to leave his family was a pile of unpaid bills.

His "rich dad" (stepfather) never finished the eighth grade, also had a substantial income, but became very wealthy. He died leaving millions of dollars to his family. The difference between the two men was their attitude about work, money, wealth and investing. His poor dad's advice was to find a job that was safe, secure and that paid a decent wage. This was his most important priority. He warned his son against taking unnecessary risks regarding entrepreneurship.

Kiyosaki's rich dad, however offered very different advice about employment. His advice was to work hard, but never rely on one's employer for one's only source of income. He advised his son to use education and opportunities to develop skills and take those skills into the market to look for ways to create his own opportunities. He taught his son to become an entrepreneur and to be willing to take reasonable risks in order to create those opportunities. Above all, he advised his son not to depend upon someone else to hand him a job.

These are two different philosophies. Both involve working, but only one is working diligently. The poor dad's advice is akin to going through the motions of swinging a pick because it is expected – not necessarily with a purpose in mind. Punch the clock. Do what is required. This is going to work day in and day out. But it is not diligence. In contrast, the rich dad's advice is akin to using the pick to mine for gold. Imagine if you were a miner that found a chunk of gold as you were swinging your pick. You think you've found a vein of gold. How diligently would you be swinging that pick to mine every single ounce of gold you could get? Nothing would stand in your way. You would swing that pick until you couldn't lift it anymore, wouldn't you? Of course you would. That's diligence.

The rich dad's advice mirrors diligence, the attitude that says, "I'll do what it takes to succeed." This is the diligence that Proverbs describes—the diligence to look for opportunities, and to do what is needed to create one's own opportunities. Diligence looks for opportunity. Diligence does what it takes to get the job done, and goes above and beyond to make sure you are doing what is necessary to save for the future.

**Principle: Persistent, hard work will pay off.**

**Life Lesson: Work diligently and save diligently.**

# 17

# LAZINESS WILL RESULT IN POVERTY

A slack hand causes poverty,
>    but the hand of the diligent makes rich. (Prov. 10:4)

The hand of the diligent will rule,
>    while the slothful will be put to forced labor. (Prov. 12:24)

At first, this principle appears to be the opposite of Chapter 16—after all, Proverbs contrasts diligence with laziness. But just as it is necessary to examine the topic of diligence, it is also necessary to dissect laziness. The topic of laziness uniquely deserves its own discussion.

> The lifestyle of laziness will destroy your long-term hopes and dreams.

Laziness is an aversion to work or being disinclined to work, or disinclined to exert activity. It is an aversion to work to the degree that it results in idleness.

Laziness is an attitude— a character trait that develops into behavior. Left unchecked it becomes a lifestyle. The lifestyle of laziness will destroy your long-term hopes and dreams. And

Proverbs offers a very simple reason why: laziness will put you in debt.

Everyone's cost of living varies, but whether you need a little or a lot, everyone needs the basics. Your need for housing, food and basic necessities will vary from that of your next-door neighbor. Whether your burn rate is slow or quick, your basic needs don't go away. They keep coming at you. Month by month by month the bills don't let up. If you are lazy, you may be able to pay your bills today, but very soon, laziness will send you into debt. And indebtedness is slavery. (Please note: by no means am I saying that people who are in debt are lazy. This is not the case at all. There are many, many legitimate reasons why hard working, diligent people find themselves in debt at some point in their career. My point is simply that if you are lazy, then you *will* end up in debt).

Why are people lazy? Yes, the common behavior of lazy people appears to be that they just won't get off their couch and work, but stop and think about it for a moment. Why won't they? What is the aversion?

Laziness is linked to a lack of character. Laziness is, or has become, part of a person's character. Like any other negative behavior, it must be dealt with head on or it will destroy one's life.

I played high school football in Oklahoma. In many parts of the country, football is just a sport. But in Oklahoma, high school football is much more; it's actually a part of the very fabric of many communities. Many young boys grow up hoping to play varsity football for their local high school. Some high school pro-grams rival those of small colleges, complete with artificial turf fields, specialized position coaches, professional trainers and tele-vised games on local cable TV stations. They can be very com-petitive, and to play on the varsity team is considered an honor and an achievement. While I was still in junior high, we had a quarterback for the varsity, Larry, who was a legitimate blue-chip prospect. He was a senior and had the tools (the skills, the size, a great arm, and the support of his high school coaches) to play Division I football at the university level. He was a pre-season

All-State selection and was even being mentioned as a potential high school All-American. His only unresolved issue in the minds of the college scouts was that he had earned a reputation for bad practice ethics (i.e., he was seen as lazy). Because of his talent, one could see how his junior high coaches may have let him slide more than some of the other kids, but in high school, he was confronted, perhaps for the first time, with his poor work ethic. The varsity coaches had no choice but to hold him to varsity standards that all the other players were held to. If he were to succeed, he would have to work hard, run sprints, and go through full speed drills just like everyone else.

Well, Larry didn't take to that very well. During summer two-a-day practices he could be heard grumbling. In his mind, he was going above and beyond to "put up with" the coaches' demands that he run sprints and go through full contact drills. But by the third or fourth game of the season, however, his complaints and constant laziness on the field became too much for the coaches to overlook. Here he was, a talented, legitimate All-State candidate. Six feet 3 inches tall with a rocket arm. But he was lazy. By the sixth game of the year, he was pulled and replaced by an in-experienced 5 feet 9 inch sophomore who was not as talented but was willing to work. The sophomore earned the starting job and Larry was benched. It was humiliating for him.

Larry promptly quit the team. After graduation, he didn't go to college or trade school, but continued to live at home and work at odd jobs. By the time I became a senior, we would often see Larry driving an old beat up car while throwing a paper route. A few years ago, a high school acquaintance told me that he saw Larry recently and that he was still doing odd jobs, mowing an occasional lawn or working sporadically only as he needed to get by. It didn't appear that Larry had come around.

Laziness is a destructive attitude that, left unchecked, becomes a lifestyle. I often wonder what would have become of Larry if he had responded to his high school coach's challenge to step up and work hard. His life could have been so different. His laziness has robbed him of so much in life.

Laziness can be, and often is, encouraged and fed unknowingly by the well-intentioned efforts of others. Hunger can be (and usually is) a healthy motivator. We are all driven by our hunger. If someone hands a lazy person what he could have only obtained through work, then the person is incentivized to be lazy. Laziness destroys your ability to fight, your desire and ability to yearn for something better. One of the largest science projects in recent memory demonstrated this vividly.

Biosphere 2 was a three-acre structure built in Arizona to explore the interactions of earth's life ecosystems in a completely controlled environment. Designed to study how man-made manipulation of the environment would affect the earth (without impacting the earth's actual atmosphere) it was the largest closed ecosystem ever created. It included a rainforest, an ocean with a coral reef, wetlands, a grassland and a fog desert.

Columbia University reported that one of the findings during its twelve-year experiment involved the wind's benefits upon plants. Wind, as we know, helps pollinate plants, spreads seeds, removes gasses that can be harmful and damaging, and can bring in different species of insects that are wind-dispersed. But, in the words of the Columbia University study, the wind also provides another crucial and even indispensable role:

> Wind is also necessary for creating hardy and strong trees. When it was first created, there was no wind inside of Biosphere 2. Plants grew relatively quickly, but they frequently fell over before they were of reproductive age. After some intensive observations and experimentation, it was determined that the lack of wind created trees with much softer wood than that species would normally make in the wild. They grew more quickly than they did in the wild, but they were harmed in the long run as a consequence.[32]

So, the wind, while inconvenient and painful to plants in their early years, helps them grow strong root systems needed to withstand the greater storms in their later years. During the early years of the Biosphere 2, its trees had been inadvertently coddled, and unknowingly allowed to be passive, or in a sense, lazy. As a result, they never developed the root system needed to survive a hostile environment. They were harmed in the long run as a consequence.

As the biosphere experiment showed, learned dependency is both subtle and deceptive. But learned dependency is also cruel. Probably no one in America's history is responsible for promoting more social welfare legislation than President Franklin Delano Roosevelt. Yet, even he understood this principle. He told Congress in his state of the union message in 1935 that, "Continued dependence upon relief induces a spiritual and moral disintegration fundamentally destructive to the national fiber. To dole out relief in this way is to administer a narcotic, a subtle destroyer of the human spirit." (1935 State of the Union Address).

Laziness, like all attitudes and behaviors, can be changed. Wisdom embraces work, labor, and even inconvenience as an opportunity to be equipped for success.

**Principle: Laziness will result in poverty.**

**Life Lesson: Learn to embrace work, labor and inconvenience so they can equip you for success.**

# 18

## DISHONEST BUSINESS PRACTICES DO NOT BRING LASTING SUCCESS

The getting of treasures by a lying tongue
    is a fleeting vapor and a snare of death. (Prov. 21:6)

Wealth gained hastily will dwindle. (Prov. 13:11a)

A false balance is an abomination to the LORD,
    but a just weight is his delight. (Prov. 11:1)

Unequal weights are an abomination to the LORD,
    and false scales are not good. (Prov. 20:23)

The getting of treasures by a lying tongue is dishonest money; Proverbs says it dwindles away. It is a fleeting vapor. Yes, by deception, dishonesty, lying, cheating and stealing you can see material gain, but ultimately it won't bring true prosperity. How can I make that claim?

It is only logical if you think about it. Your company's integrity is vital. Your suppliers, employees, and ultimately your customers, must be able to trust you. If you cheat, lie or engage in unethical business practices, you jeopardize that trust and run the risk of ultimately destroying the very foundation upon which your company rests.

But there is another more subtle, underlying, and unseen reason that this proverb is true. You see, when you bend the rules to get wealth, you poison your ability to enjoy what you have obtained. You sabotage that which you are trying to achieve.

Why do people bend the rules? To get ahead. To achieve. So they can have more. Acquiring more possessions improves the quality of life, right? Perhaps for a time, but the truth is that if you cheat to get money it will not satisfy you. Acquiring it illegally or unethically brings guilt and paranoia. Specifically it brings:

> When you bend the rules to get wealth, you poison your ability to enjoy what you have obtained.

1.  The guilt of having cheated another person

2.  The fear of discovery and prosecution

3.  The fear of possible of retaliation by your victim

This toxic combination of guilt and fear causes stress that nags and irritates, preventing us from experiencing the enjoyment that money earned honestly can bring. This is why Proverbs 28:1 declares, "The wicked flee when no one pursues, but the righteous are bold as a lion."

> Always having to look over your shoulder is no way to live.

Always having to look over your shoulder is no way to live. Living a life inherently laced with stress and anxiety, uncomfortable with guilt and fear of getting caught, and without peace of mind is no way to live. Yet so many are trying to do just that.

When God Himself abhors and detests the methods by which you are operating, that is, to say the least, not a place of comfort and peace. If this describes your business practices, then you are not operating under God's favor, and you cannot enjoy His blessing. In fact, you are setting yourself up for Him to discipline you, and this is a dangerous place to be. God's judgment is not a popular topic. A believer in Jesus, who is a new creature in Christ, is not under eternal condemnation for his sins anymore, but God will not honor and bless his business if he is operating in deception. Operating one's business unethically takes that business out from under God's umbrella of favor and exposes him to whatever may come. This is dangerous.

> Operating one's business unethically takes that business out from under God's umbrella of favor and exposes him to whatever may come. This is dangerous.

Many people think they can live anyway they want to and that there are no consequences for their actions. After all, you see the wicked "prospering" every day. Yes, unethical people can and often do prosper for a season, but prosperity that comes as a result of evil, deception, and dishonesty is fleeting and will be brought down. You may or may not live to see the negative consequences, but they will come.

Life has a way of testing what is true. It has a way of flushing out deception. Bernard Madoff was able to bilk investors on Wall Street out of millions for a long time, but his deception eventually caught up to him. Today he sits in ruin. We see the landscape littered with similar examples of those operating their businesses in the shadows of deception.

There is an inherent factor regarding dishonesty and corruption that will display itself. A person may be able to fool people, even a lot of people for a long time, but life has a way of validating what is accurate and true. And life has a way of invalidating what is based upon deception. There will be consequences, regardless of whether one's lack of integrity is publicly demonstrated and made known to those around them. Proverbs accentuates this point:

> Whoever walks in integrity walks securely,
>> but he who makes his ways crooked will be found out.
> Whoever winks the eye causes trouble,
>> and a babbling fool will come to ruin. (Prov. 10:9-10)

> The prudent sees danger and hides himself,
>> but the simple go on and suffer for it. (Prov. 22:3)

Cheating in business is quite common. Research shows that one of the most common ways that Americans cheat in both their businesses and in their private lives is by not reporting income on their taxes. Another common way is by over valuing their tax deductions. Among the most common methods of cheating in commercial businesses is doctoring products to make them deceptively appealing or to appear of higher quality than they really are. Yet another prominent method of cheating in business is taking advantage of customers who are unfamiliar or ignorant of products or services. Auto repair facilities can suffer terrible reputations for these practices because customers believe they are often sold services that are not needed.

Customers appreciate full disclosure. And generally, they will reward businesses that place a priority on integrity and high-quality customer service. Probably the leading retail establishment in the nation in the area of customer service is Nordstrom's department stores. Started in 1901, the chain of high-end fashion stores is renowned for its impeccable customer service. Their employee handbook is one page long. It lists their one value as "use good judgment at all times" and their one priority is "please the customer." They are straight shooters, and customers acknowledge that by giving Nordstrom their repeat business. Nordstrom's executives believe it is a chief reason that they enjoy $5 billion in sales annually. People will reward ethical businesses with their patronage. But businesses that don't practice ethical behavior suffer.

Corruption in business also takes its toll on society at large, which hurts all of us. Medicare fraud costs our nation $60 billion per year (many sources cite much higher figures) and has contributed to our runaway deficits and our staggering national debt. That's $200 per year for every man, woman and child, or $700 per family. But it actually costs more because that money is borrowed money that the government is paying interest on, so it really costs $735 (at 5% interest).

Identity theft costs Americans $56 billion per year. About nine million Americans will be victims of identity theft each year. And we all pay for it, as the credit card companies pass on their losses through higher interest rates. So that's another $700 per family.

Illegal alien workers may increase profits for their employers, but they are costing the American taxpayer upwards of $70 billion per year. Most of the estimated fifteen million illegal aliens work for low wages, often in the underground economy and pay little or no taxes on their earnings. You, the U.S taxpayer, pay to educate children of illegal aliens, pay for their health care through Medicaid, and pay to incarcerate them when they commit crimes. These costs are passed on to you and me through higher taxes. So that's another $800 per family.

One of the greatest tragedies of illegal immigration is that the illegals are vulnerable to becoming victims. Because they are underground, they resist reporting crimes against them. Abuse and victimization are common in this community. They are caught in the shadows and are at the mercy of those that employ them illegally. The employer is knowingly violating the law, so the employer and the employee are operating in the shadows, which is not good for either of them. It is not good for the workers it displaces, our school systems, our hospitals, or our correctional facilities. It is not good for our society.

These are just three of the dishonest business practices that are hurting our society. And these three alone are costing each American family $2,200 per year. We as a nation are just now beginning to understand that we are indeed paying a terrible price for these unethical business practices.

If you want to be wise, follow the advice of Proverbs and operate your business with honesty and integrity.

**Principle: Dishonest business practices
do not bring lasting success.**

**Life Lesson: Conduct your business
with honesty and integrity.**

# 19

# YOUR REPUTATION IS MORE VALUABLE THAN YOUR POSSESSIONS

A good name is to be chosen rather than great riches,
and favor is better than silver or gold. (Prov. 22:1)

A reputation is better than money? Come on. That's just a quaint catch phrase, right? No. Your reputation is indeed more valuable than money.

Let me show you.

Technology can actually measure your reputation. In fact, it can even track your reputation (or measure it over time). When a political candidate is first considering running for office, one of the first and most important issues that he must first take into consideration is his name identification (ID). This measures a simple answer to the question, "How many people have heard of you?" Within this measurement is whether people have a favorable or unfavorable opinion of the candidate. An incumbent office holder should have decent name ID since he or she has been on the ballot in previous elections. If the office holder has worked diligently in office and has decent relations with the press, he or she will usually have a significantly higher "favorable" than "unfavorable" number. A poll that shows 75% hard name ID with 55% favorable and 15% unfavorable (and 5% no opinion) is an example of an incumbent who will cruise to re-election.

This is the first benchmark measurement that is taken when any campaign begins because it determines how challenging the race will be. Why? Because the basic rule in politics is *better the devil we do know, than the devil we don't.* In other words, *people won't vote for someone they've never heard of.* They just won't. In the voting booth, they will skip that race and go down the ballot and pull the lever for the races or candidates they are familiar with.

Most challengers or first-time candidates seeking open seats (where no incumbent is running for re-election) do not have very high name ID. If they do have some name ID, it is usually soft, which means that people may have heard of the candidate's name, but don't really know who they are or what they stand for. It is extremely rare for a challenger to have either hard name ID or a high favorable opinion. That kind of name ID is rare and valuable in today's culture. And if you don't start out with name ID and you want to win your race, you must buy it. Yes, you can buy a good reputation. But as any good media consultant will tell you, it takes a sophisticated combination of time, a deliberate and consistent media strategy, and a huge boatload of money to buy a favorable reputation.

In a small state it will cost several hundred thousand dollars to bump up your name ID, and hundreds of thousands more to bump up your favorables. In a large state, it costs millions. Because they start out with high name ID (and often decent favorables) professional athletes and celebrities (even C or D list celebrities) make intriguing candidates for political office. Starting out with high favorables in a large (and expensive) state like California, New York, Texas or Florida can be worth $10 million in advertising. With high name ID and high favorables, you are instantly competitive.

If a candidate has high unfavorables (i.e., a bad reputation) then the money needed to turn those numbers into high favorables and low unfavorables multiplies. The campaign gets really expensive, really fast. So, give me two candidates, one with a sterling reputation and the ability to raise a decent amount of money and another with a bad reputation but a huge wallet, and I'll put my money on the candidate with a good reputation every time. In many cases, the candidate with the bad reputation cannot spend enough to turn public opinion in his favor. So in politics, a good reputation is literally worth more than silver and gold.

How we behave, how we treat people, how we speak to them, what we value—in essence who we are—can be shaped or spun to some people. But, in the end, most people will see and know the reality, regardless of how much we try to spin.

One of my favorite films is Frank Capra's classic Christmas film, *It's a Wonderful Life.* The villain in the film, crusty old Henry Potter, had more money than anyone in town. But all of his money could not buy what George Bailey had. George Bailey had hundreds of friends. Both on an individual level and collectively, he enjoyed a genuine appreciation and affection from the entire community. And in having this, he actually had both money (since they all passed the hat to pay off Bailey's debt) and the love of the community. In the movie's final scene, Jimmy Sterwart's character George Bailey realizes the truth of Proverbs 22:1 when someone exclaims, "There's George Bailey... the richest man in town." The look on Jimmy Stewart's face when he realizes the truth of that statement is priceless. It's a great ending to a wonderful film. The power of that message is one of the reasons that the film has become such a timeless classic.

A good reputation creates opportunities and draws people to you. Your reputation precedes you. Some people know you personally, but many, many more know you by reputation.

How does a person get a good reputation? A reputation takes time to develop. It's not something one just decides to establish overnight. It's the sum total of one's values, intentions, work product, and most importantly, one's relationships. And yes, it's established by the words we use and the actions we take, but it's also crafted by the things we don't do, and the things we don't say. It's established by the way we treat others. Our actions speak louder than our words. Our reputation either validates what we hope others know of us, or it steps on what we want oth-

> Regardless of what we want others to know of us, over time life has a way of testing what we are really made of, what we really believe, and who we are.

ers to know of us. What Proverbs is trying to tell us is this: Regardless of what we want others to know of us, over time life has a way of testing what we are really made of, what we really believe, and who we are.

This is why Proverbs instructs us to *live consistently* with the understanding that our words and our actions are generally available for all to see. Over time our true selves will be shown for all to see.

**Principle: Your reputation is more valuable than your possessions.**

**Life Lesson: Protect your reputation by living consistently.**

# 20

# THERE IS NO SHORTCUT TO WEALTH

A faithful man will abound with blessings,
   but whoever hastens to be rich will not go unpunished.
   (Prov. 28:20)

"Making haste" describes an attitude of impatience, the kind that involves suspending one's usual judgment and taking risks, cutting corners, or compromising one's values. It describes not just the willingness but also the tenacious desire to find a shortcut to wealth. In modern language, this proverb is warning against get-rich-quick-schemes. What is a get-rich-quick-scheme? What distinguishes it from a legitimate investment opportunity? A get-rich-quick scheme involves any idea or plan that promises that very little time, effort, or skill is required in return for a profit.

A successful endeavor will involve the legitimate creation of value and will almost always require inconvenience and labor. This is based upon Proverbs 14:4:

Where there are no oxen, the manger is clean,
but abundant crops come by the strength of the ox.

Profit results when value is created. In other words, gain is a result of providing skills or needed goods and services at a competitive price. Profit can also be gained from adding value to an existing good or service. Profit can also be earned from providing attention to detail and good customer service. These are the inconveniences and messes referred to in Proverbs 14:4 involving effort, labor, organizational skill, and attention to detail. They're not pretty or fun, but they are the inherent and necessary ingredients required to see a profit. Again, not exciting, but effective.

> A successful endeavor will involve the legitimate creation of value and will almost always require inconvenience and labor.

Our culture values immediacy. We want and sometimes can have instant access to just about everything. But as much as we might hope or think otherwise, there is no instant access to wealth.

Certainly, quick profits hold an attraction for everyone, and most of us at some point have entertained the idea of an aggressive investment or plan to make quick money. Some people spend their lives looking for that one short cut, that one key to instant wealth, or that one golden opportunity for which they might suspend their better judgment because it's "such a great opportunity." For many it's the lottery. These are the efforts Proverbs warns against.

Earlier we looked at the wealth accumulated over time by the person that invests one dollar per day. Starting with $1,000, (and gaining 6% interest) he would have about $1,450 in one year, $3,500 in five years and $96,000 in forty-five years. Let's look at how that same person would fare if instead of saving that dollar, he spent it on a lottery ticket. Buying one $1 lottery ticket each day, in one year he would have spent $365. In five years he would have spent $1,825 and in forty-five years he would have spent $16, 425. Of course, there is always that million to one chance that he'd have hit the jackpot, but his chances of doing that are just that... one in a million.

The odds in gambling are inherently against us. The business model of casinos is based upon this fact. Casino owners understand that even if customers do win, if they stay and keep playing, they (the owners) will get back all of the money their gambling customers paid and more. The person who is able to become wealthy through gambling is very rare.

How is wealth defined? What makes a person wealthy? The dictionary defines wealth as an abundance or a plentiful amount. Each of us has a different idea of what wealth is. For some having $100,000 would be enough to consider themselves wealthy. For many, it would take a million or many millions. I personally would consider a person wealthy if they were able to eliminate all debt, pay any ongoing expenses such as utilities, food, insurance, etc. without having to work (being able to live off of the interest of their investments) and having enough left over for charitable giving and a few luxuries, such as vacations. Wealthy would mean being able to spend their time doing what they want to do.

People usually become wealthy in one or some combination of the following ways:

1.  Hard work and saving (and investing) over time;

2.  Having a unique value or an exclusive possession (talent, skill, intellectual property, software, etc) that is brought to the market to meet consumer demand;

3.  Leveraging the skills of others, or adding value to the skills or services of others;

4. Marketing the skills and services of others to a larger audience or customer base;

5. Inheritance (to be an heir is a blessing as you are the beneficiary of someone else's hard word and perseverance).

Almost every person who has become wealthy has used one or more of these methods. This is the way wealth is built.

It's a big world and a big market. There are a variety of needs and many opportunities for becoming wealthy. Education, skills, creativity, hard work, discipline and perseverance can take you a long way toward your financial goals. Shortcuts are not wise. Those who seek them out will more often than not pay a steep price.

**Principle: There is no shortcut to wealth.**

**Life Lesson: Establish a financial strategy based on reasonable expectations, not through presumption or schemes that require no time, effort or money.**

# 21

# DON'T CONTRACTUALLY OBLIGATE YOURSELF ON BEHALF OF OTHERS

Proverbs has a great deal to say about this topic:

> My son, if you have put up security for your neighbor, have given your pledge for a stranger, if you are snared in the words of your mouth, caught in the words of your mouth, then do this, my son, and save yourself, for you have come into the hand of your neighbor: go, hasten, and plead urgently with your neighbor. Give your eyes no sleep and your eyelids no slumber, save yourself like a gazelle from the hand of the hunter, like a bird from the hand of the fowler. (6:1-5)

> Whoever puts up security for a stranger will surely suffer harm, but he who hates striking hands in pledge is secure. (11:15)

One who lacks sense gives a pledge
    and puts up security in the presence of his neighbor.
    (Prov. 17:18)

Take a man's garment when he has put up security for a
    stranger. (Prov. 20:16a)

Be not one of those who give pledges, who put up
    security for debts.
If you have nothing with which to pay,
    why should your bed be taken from under you?
    (Prov. 22:26-27)

Take a man's garment when he has put up security for a
    stranger. (Prov. 27:13a)

Some scholars may argue that Proverbs offers slight distinc-
tions between circumstances depending upon the nature of the
relationship between the lender and the borrower, and that the
warnings regarding loaning to a neighbor are not as stern as the
warning against loaning to a stranger. However, the text doesn't
support the distinction between how neighbors and strangers are
to be treated because it warns against taking the obligations of
both. On the contrary, it explicitly warns that taking on another's
obligation may result in losing all you have worked for.

    One could make the case that this prohibition doesn't neces-
sarily apply to family members. Most parents, this one included
have a hard time standing by and watching a child or close loved
one placed at risk due to unfortunate circumstances. Wisdom, I
believe would dictate that if one does agree to become surety for
a family member, only do so with the understanding that you may
very well be required to pay the obligation, and co-sign only if
you are prepared to be the one that pays it back.

    Always keep in mind that by accepting responsibility for
another person's loans, you are placing yourself in a situation

over which you have no control. Solomon emphatically urges that agreeing to be security for another's debt should be avoided and a person should do whatever it takes to free himself from the obligation, even if it means great humiliation or obnoxious pleading.

Again, these are general principles by which each of us should operate in our daily lives and our businesses. Emergencies and unforeseen loss are often addressed through insurance, which operates on the principle of indemnification. To indemnify is to guard against anticipated loss. In the insurance industry, teams of data analysts calculate degrees of risk involved and help people take responsibility and share their risks. In these cases, the obligations are not entered into haphazardly or without just consideration of the risks involved. Indeed, the risks are well accounted for and mathematically factored into actuarial tables with the premiums adjusted accordingly. Risk sharing programs, such as shared medical expenses / indemnification programs can provide an alternative to traditional insurance. These industries are highly regulated, which further mitigate risks for those participating. Neither insurance, shared medical expense programs, nor the surety industry run afoul of Proverbs' admonition against co-signing loans because these arrangements forsee potential difficulties and prepare in advance for them.

The appropriate application from Proverbs is that one should only co-sign a loan if you can afford—and are fully prepared—to be the one that pays it off.

**Principle: Don't contractually obligate yourself on behalf of others.**

**Life Lesson: Only co-sign a loan if you can afford (and are fully prepared) to be the one that pays it off.**

# 22

# KEEP MONEY IN PERSPECTIVE

**M**oney. We all need it. We all want it—and lots of it. Come on, admit it. You want more money. If you say you don't, then you're probably lying. There's nothing wrong with wanting more money. You need money to live. And you probably need more than you have right now. You have to eat. You need money to pay your bills. Your kids need new shoes, your car is overdue for maintenance and your kids need to go to college. So don't feel guilty about needing more money. Most of us need more money than we have.

> Don't feel guilty about needing more money. Most of us need more money than we have.

Because we need it, all of us in our own way are working to get more money. But, according to Proverbs, it's *how* we go about it that makes all the difference. Proverbs gives guidelines and offers specific warnings about the way that we engage in our work. And it actually gives very good advice on *how* to engage in the effort for more money.

First, Proverbs warns against focusing on money – against setting as the goal of our lives, or as one of the goals of our lives, the acquisition of money, and the things money can buy. If you have set the acquisition of a set amount of money as a major goal, then it captivates your attention, your actions, and determines your priorities. Making money is a necessary activity that we must undertake, but it must not determine our priorities. Instead, our priorities should determine the parameters around which we conduct our affairs, including how and where we work.

Your life's purpose is not to acquire. You are made for much more noble purposes than to acquire and collect things. (We'll expound more on that in the upcoming chapters).

> Do not toil to acquire wealth; be discerning enough to desist. When your eyes light on it, it is gone, for suddenly it sprouts wings, flying like an eagle toward heaven. (Prov. 23:4-5)

When you set your eyes on gaining wealth and focus on getting more money, your perspective changes. And therein is the danger of becoming materialistic. It's easy to do, especially in our society where everything seems so readily available and within our reach. Becoming motivated by materialism is very, very easy to do. What is being materialistic? Living materialistically is when we make money the goal. And this is wrong, because when money is the goal, then the chase for it becomes the purpose of our lives.

> Anytime we set as a goal the acquisition of money, we look past the moment, the now, the people and circumstances in the moment, in exchange for what lies beyond our reach. We look beyond the now for a fantasy.

How do you know if you're being materialistic? If you define your goals in life by an amount of money that you are trying to acquire, or by specific things that you must have, then you are probably being materialistic. If you think about it for a moment, it is foolish to do that. Why? Because anytime we set as a goal the acquisition of money, we look past the moment, the now, the people and circumstances in the moment in exchange for what lies beyond our reach. We look beyond the now for a fantasy, which may or may not even exist in the future.

Once we develop this way of thinking, it becomes our way of life. It is our lifestyle. We become entrenched in the chase.

How many people have lived that lifestyle of focusing all their energy on making money to the exclusion of other things in life, only to find out that it left them hollow? Brian "Head" Welch is one such person. The lead guitarist of the rock band "Korn" explains,

> "My dream came true... I made more money, I played bigger shows, houses, cars, I tried drugs, I tried sex, I tried everything to try to get pleasure out of this life and I thought I could fulfill my life with all this stuff, but it didn't fulfill it...."[33]

Brian saw the foolishness of chasing money. Even when you get it, it cannot truly satisfy. He discovered a profound truth, which is attributed to humorist Art Buchwald, "The best things in life aren't things."[34]

God wants us to live in the now—in the moment. He wants us to be sensitive to the needs of others around us. He wants us to be responsive to His whisper. This moment is the only one over which you have any control. You are not guaranteed that next year, next month, next week, or even that tomorrow will ever come.

If the only time you realize this is after you've reached the goal, then you've wasted the most valuable commodity you have:

your time. You will have spent your life pursuing something that doesn't satisfy. Solomon discovered this. Solomon had more money than he could spend and it left

> Solomon had more money than he could spend and it left him empty.

him empty, seeking meaning in a wide variety of pursuits, sending him searching to find a deeper sense of fulfillment.

So we all need money to live, and we see that Proverbs holds that it is wise to work diligently to provide for our families and ourselves. But acquiring money shouldn't be the goal of life. So if money isn't the goal in life, what is? Proverbs addresses this, and so will we, later in this book.

**Principle: Keep money in perspective.**

**Life Lesson: Don't make the acquisition of money or possessions the goal of your life.**

# 23

# GENEROUS PEOPLE WILL BENEFIT FROM THEIR GENEROSITY

Proverbs encourages generosity:

Whoever brings blessing will be enriched,
and one who waters will himself be watered.
(Prov. 11:25)

Whoever has a bountiful eye will be blessed,
for he shares his bread with the poor. (Prov. 22:9)

Whoever closes his ear to the cry of the poor will himself
call out and not be answered. (Prov. 21:13)

Likewise, the stingy will not be cared for by others.
(Prov. 21:13).

The way you treat others will come back to you. It's a basic principle found in many faiths; Christianity, Judaism, Buddhism, Hinduism, and Confucianism.[35] In Proverbs, Solomon teaches that if you are generous, your generosity will come back to you. Proverbs is not describing some kind of Coke machine formula, whereby you are generous once and it will come back to you immediately. Rather Solomon is describing a pattern seen throughout the course of one's life. He is describing a way of life. The person who lives a lifestyle of generous giving will be known as a kind and giving person. And generous people elicit good will and generosity from others. Those that are known to readily give to others are able to find help when they themselves have needs.

Generous giving is important because it demonstrates your priorities. In Matthew 6:21 Jesus said, "For where your treasure is, there your heart will be also." In other words, where your dollars go will demonstrate where your affections lie. What you spend your money on demonstrates your priorities. It proves your values. A former mentor used to say to me, "What you believe is what you do... everything else is just religious talk."

I believe this is true. According to Jesus, the way you spend your money indicates your priorities. In America, most people who say they believe the Bible really don't believe this. If they did, they would give more money away.

American Christians give away relatively little money. More than 25% of Protestants don't give away any money at all. 32% of Evangelicals give away at least 2% of their income annually. About 27% of Evangelicals tithe (which is 10 per cent of take home after-tax income). Interestingly, the poorest Christians give away more per capita than the middle class, and the wealthiest Christians actually give away the largest percentage of their income.[36]

Christianity Today examined the giving habits of Christians in America and found that America's Christians that say their religion is very important to them and go to church at least twice per month earn more than $2.5 trillion annually. This makes American Christians the seventh largest economy in the world. The article pointed out that if these believers gave away 10% of their after tax earnings it would funnel an additional $46 billion into ministry, which would be a remarkable and noticeable infusion of resources into charitable Christian causes. Here are some of the changes such giving could produce:

- $10 billion would sponsor 20 million children living in squalor and without the gospel

- $330 million would sponsor 150,000 indigenous missionaries in closed countries

- $2.2 billion would triple the current funding for Bible translation and distribution, and

- $660 million would start eight Christian colleges in Eastern Europe and Southeast Asia

One's giving to others, the needy in particular, is certainly one of the most important indicators of one's values. Where your treasure is, there will your heart be also.

An example of a generous giver is Seymour Schulich, founder of Franco-Nevada Mining Corp. One of Canada's wealthiest people, he is worth nearly $2 billion, and has given hundreds of millions to charities. He is the author of *Get Smarter: Life and Business Lessons.* He has written about the satisfaction gained from giving. "Money is like fertilizer: if you pile it up, it stinks, and if you spread it around, you can grow some beautiful things."[37]

Generous philanthropy benefits society. It benefits you and me. At the turn of this century some of the new Internet billionaires began to donate significant amounts of money to medical research. Until that time an increased pool of money had only been available through the rigorous and often tedious rubric of government regulations. The progress in medical research as a result of this rapid infusion of new cash was felt so quickly that some medical research insiders began discussing reforms in federal grant making processes to reflect the methodology of these new philanthropists.

We in the West have been given much. We are expected to give to those less fortunate, and we should. We should be generous givers. If you want to be wise, incorporate generous giving into your life. I know what you are thinking. "There is no way that I can do that. I can't afford it." Fair enough. I understand completely. Believe me I do. I put five kids through college, so I understand how expensive life is.

### *But I want to encourage you to consider doing two things:*

First, try this experiment. Test it to see if it works. Once you have completed your household budget mentioned in Chapter 15, set up automatic withdrawal from your checking account each month that will go into a savings account. Be sure to set it up for automatic withdrawal, even if it's for a token amount, even if it's $3 a month. Arrange to have that amount automatically set aside in savings. Once that account reaches $15, give it to a noble and honorable charity that serves the less fortunate. Five months later, when the amount reaches $15, then do it again. And do it every five months, each time the amount reaches $15. Send it to Compassion International to sponsor a child for one month, or give it to your local church. What matters is that you do something. If and when you prosper, increase the amount to 5$ or $10 per month. Test it. See if you don't benefit from it.

Second, I want you to teach your kids how to give generously. Practice it with them. Try this exercise: Give them a few dollars and tell them they have to spend it on others. They are not allowed to spend it on themselves. Tell them to take notes on their actions; track who they give the money to and where it goes. Repeat the process a few times. Then talk with your kids about how it feels to give money away and about the lessons they are learning from the process. It will provide an opportunity to discuss the value of money, the value of work, and their feelings as they encounter people in poverty and want. It is a prime opportunity to teach them to become generous givers. It is a great opportunity to teach them that indeed generous people will be blessed.

**Principle: Generous people will benefit
from their generosity.**

**Life Lesson: Become a generous giver.
You will benefit from it.**

PART V

# SPIRITUALITY

# 24

# THE FEAR OF THE LORD IS THE BEGINNING OF WISDOM

The fear of the LORD is the beginning of wisdom,
and the knowledge of the Holy One is insight.
(Prov. 9:10)

What is the "fear of the Lord?" At first glance, one might think this verse expects you to live cowering in fear of a God that is waiting to thump you every time you make a mistake. Sadly, many people do have this impression of God, but it is not accurate.

The truth is quite different.

There are several Hebrew words used in Scripture for "fear." One is *eymah (ay-mah)* which is the kind of fear associated with horror and fright. Another is *pachad (paw-kkad)* which means to be startled or shocked as when you are surprised. The "fear" mentioned here in Proverbs is *yir-ah (yir-aw)* which means reverent or reverence.

The "fear of the Lord" means a reverence and respect for God, for His law, and for His sovereignty over your life. This is why the amplified Bible translates Proverbs 9:10:

> The reverent fear of the Lord, that is, worshiping Him and regarding Him as truly awesome, is the beginning and preeminent part of wisdom, its starting point and its essence.

It is entirely consistent for a child to love his parents dearly, to know that his parents love him and care for him, and at the same time fear the consequences of disobedience to them. He knows that their requirements upon him are not arbitrary or menacing. He understands that they are for his benefit, and he understands that if he chooses to disobey his parents, there will be consequences that are redemptive in nature, intended for his correction to help him learn to obey. Reverence of this type is appropriate.

Okay, living with a healthy respect for God and His laws is important, but why does Proverbs say that reverence for God is the *beginning* of wisdom? Because true wisdom starts with acknowledging God—that He exists, and that He is your creator.

It is only in the context of obedience to God that Proverbs works as intended. It is the foundational principle that puts the rest of the book in its proper context. Wisdom starts with acknowledging Him as the source of all life. The appropriate view of God acknowledges that He is your creator, and that as His creation you are dependent upon Him

> It is only in the context of obedience to God that Proverbs works as intended.

for your sustenance. It means acknowledging that He is the supplier of your needs, and as such that you are dependent upon Him. If you think about it a moment, it basically means that you live your life in agreement with God's view of reality. You live with the understanding that He is, and He is sovereign over you. Eugene Peterson's popular translation of the Bible entitled *The Message* translates Proverbs 9:10:

> Skilled living gets its start in the Fear-of-God, insight into life from knowing a Holy God.

Solomon's father David wrote in Psalm 14:1: "The fool says in his heart, 'There is no God.'" More than any other trait, denying the existence of one's creator is the single most important criteria to determine whether one moves toward the path of wisdom or toward a path that reaches foolish conclusions and consequences. Isn't this narrow minded? No, it's not. You see, Proverbs is much more than a list of "do's and don'ts," or a list of suggestions or "best courses of action." It is not a list of boxes to check that will somehow insure success. It is not intended to be a self-help book. It is not that. Yes, it serves as a set of guidelines, and a list of very practical principles for living, but it is intended to speak to us *in the context of our relationship to our Creator.* It *assumes* that we are living in a specified relationship to our creator. A man who had a genuine, dynamic, substantive relationship with God wrote Proverbs. And it was written to a people that were living in relationship with God.

Even in the New Testament, people who are living in covenant relationship with God are described in Acts 9:31 as living "in the fear of the Lord." Reverence for God is the foundation for a solid life.

> The fear of the Lord is the beginning of knowledge...
>     (Prov. 1:7a)

> The Fear of the Lord is instruction in wisdom, and
>     humility comes before honor. (Prov. 15:33)

The book of Proverbs is meant for those pursuing a relationship with Him, as both Solomon and David did. Remember that King Solomon's wisdom was given to him *after* he sought God's will for his new kingdom. Solomon's gaining of wisdom was a result of his personal relationship with God. It was an answer to prayer—the result of his asking God for it. And God granted it to him.

In 1 Kings 3:9, 11-12, the newly crowned King Solomon prays,

> Give your servant therefore an understanding mind to govern your people, that I may discern between good and evil, for who is able to govern this your great people?" (1 Kings 3:9)

> And God said to him, "Because you have asked this, and have not asked for yourself long life or riches or the life of your enemies, but have asked for yourself understanding to discern what is right, 12 behold, I now do according to your word. Behold, I give you a wise and discerning mind, so that none like you has been before you and none like you shall arise after you. (1 Kings 3:11-12)

He received wisdom that was renowned throughout the known world.

You can follow the principles in this book and make quality decisions in daily life regarding finances, relationships, and personal development; but if you aren't recognizing God and your responsibilities toward him, Proverbs says that you will not be truly wise because you

> Proverbs says that you never will be truly wise... until you recognize... that He is the source of... life, and you acknowledge your obligations to Him.

will have missed the bigger, eternal picture. You'll be *minoring on the majors* and *majoring on the minors*.

In fact, Proverbs says that you never will be truly wise, as the Bible defines wisdom, until you recognize that God exists and that He is the source of all wisdom. Wisdom will elude you until you recognize that He is not just the source of life, but that He is the source of *your* life, and you acknowledge your obligations to Him.

What are your obligations toward God? How does one appropriately "fear" God? It is one of the most important questions you will ever answer, and the subject of our next chapter.

**Principle: The fear of the Lord is
the beginning of wisdom.**

**Life Lesson: Bow your knee in humble
acknowledgement that God is sovereign over you.**

# 25

# GOD IS ULTIMATELY IN CONTROL

The king's heart is a stream of water in the hand of the Lord; he turns it wherever he will. (Prov. 21:1)

God is sovereign. Nothing happens that He does not allow. *Wait a minute,* you ask, *God is in control? Well, that can't be.... what about evil in the world?* If God is in control, then why do such bad things happen? Surely such a loving God wouldn't allow such evil. Either God is not in control or He is evil. How else can you account for the suffering?

Fair questions. Let's look for answers together. Scripture says that God is love, and that His love is limitless. Lamentations 3:22-23 tells us that the Lord's great love and compassions never fail; they are new every morning. In His love for us He gave us the ultimate dignity: the ability to choose to serve Him. Inherent in that choice is the ability to reject Him. And when He did that He knew it would result in some, even many, choosing not to follow Him.

We were created in the context of a cosmic battle between God and Satan. Good and evil. This means that you have an enemy who hates you. Satan hates you, and he hates your Creator. He hates who you are, but mostly he fears who you are designed to become. When Adam was created, he was a prince, given authority to rule as God's regent on the earth. He had dominion over it. He ruled it. He named the animals. He cared for the garden. He was *the man*.

So the enemy came after the man to take him out. He deceived both Adam and Eve, and they surrendered that authority and dominion that had been designated to them to Satan. God had created man and woman with the ability to choose obedience, with the ability to walk in their designed place of regency, but they voluntarily handed that dominion and authority over to Satan.

The impact on the human race was profound. As a result of their fall came guilt, shame, pain, death, alienation from God, and the need for atonement and redemption. The earth was impacted as well. Satan became the regent. And it is his regency, his rule in this world that is the source of evil. Man is born fallen from his original status, and in significant ways, under Satan's influence. Because of this, man's natural inclination is to perpetuate the rejection of God's love to pursue his own selfish ends, which often include hurting other people. Greed, malice, slander and cruelty became our inclination, our predisposition.

Yes, God knew it would happen. And no, it didn't catch Him by surprise. Before the creation of the world, God knew that the human race would fall and would stand in need of redemption. He knew we would need restoration and salvation. And so He destined to achieve that redemption even before he created Adam and Eve with the capacity to choose evil.

So God knew there would be pain and suffering. He knew that there would be millions of people that would ultimately reject His love, and who would, by their own choices, miss the destiny that God designed for them. Yet, He created us anyway. In the counsels of His own wisdom, He determined that this terrible cost was the price of you and me having freedom. So even though God knew of the pain that *He* would suffer and the pain that *we* would suffer, He determined that it is worth it.

When we look at life from this Biblical perspective, it makes sense. God is in control. And in His control, He has designated lines of dignity that He will honor—your choices. Your will, your choices are the only areas in the universe where God has voluntarily limited His authority and His sovereignty. And He has done so in recognition of your dignity. He has done so as an act of love toward you.

You may be thinking, *but wait a minute; I thought you said that nothing happens that God doesn't allow.* So if God has voluntarily limited His control over us, how can He still be in control? How can He be sovereign? How can a verse like Proverbs 21:1 "The king's heart is a stream of water in the hand of the Lord; he turns it wherever he will" be true?

> Your will, your choices are the only areas in the universe where God has voluntarily limited His authority and His sovereignty. And He has done so in recognition of your dignity. He has done so as an act of love toward you.

It is mysterious. Even in His self-imposed limitation, He still exercises authority to influence our decisions. Throughout history we see how God speaks, encourages, woos, warns, and moves miraculously to demonstrate His power to us—all to woo us to follow and trust Him. Jonah ran from God, but God still got him to Nineveh. God hardened Pharaoh's heart so that Pharaoh wouldn't let the Israelites leave Egypt. Time and again, God intervened and caused armies to turn on themselves in confusion and kill each other. God called out Saul of Tarsus (the man who persecuted the early church leaders) to become Paul the Apostle, the apostle to the non-Jewish world. God confronted him directly—literally knocked him off of his horse, and changed the man in an instant. God didn't violate Saul's free will, yet in His wisdom He knew what it would take to change Saul's heart so He did it.

Nothing is outside God's ultimate control. God controls governing authorities. He can and will orchestrate events, even the overthrow of governments, kingdoms, princes, and rulers. He is sovereign over all rulers. Yes, He has created us with the ability to be like Him; to create, to choose, and to have dominion. Yes, we have yielded that authority to our spiritual enemy who hates us. So yes, bad things happen. And they will continue to happen until God's rule and authority is consummated at the end of the age. But God is still in control.

You may hear someone ask, "If God exists, what is He doing? Why can't we have more evidence of His existence and of what He's doing today?" I would submit to you that He has given us clear and unambiguous revelation of Himself and of His purposes. And the short answer is that He is (and has been) actively and purposefully moving to reconcile the world to Himself. This includes you. If you are not a student of history, all you need is to open a book and look around to see God's hand that has moved throughout history to redeem this world to Himself. One can only understand what's happening around you if you understand the context in which it's taking place. Only when you understand the context of where you (and we as humankind) have been, can you understand where you are and where you are heading. If you have never studied the Bible, I encourage you to do so. God's hand in redemptive history is there for you to discover.

So what does this mean to you? Turn to the next chapter and read on.

### Principle: God is in control.

### Life Lesson: God is moving in and through events to accomplish His purposes.

# 26

# TRUST GOD WITH YOUR FUTURE

Trust in the LORD with all your heart, and do not lean on your own understanding. In all your ways acknowledge him, and he will make straight your paths. (Prov. 3:5-6)

Foundational to any relationship is trust. Without it, there really can be no relationship. Whether between husband and wife, between family members, or between two friends—that simple trust is the basis for everything else in the relationship. If it doesn't exist, there is no foundation upon which to build. In your relationship with God, there is no more important element than trust. Scripture is very, very clear that without trust in God there can be no relationship with Him.

> Without trust in God there can be no relationship with Him.

And without faith it is impossible to please him, for whoever would draw near to God must believe that he exists
and that he rewards those who seek him. (Heb. 11:6)

But so many people in our culture today are unsure of God and
His existence. How can you trust in something you don't see? You
can't see Him, so how can you believe in Him, much less trust Him?

It is asking a lot, isn't it? Trusting in something you can't
see? But if you think about it, we do it every day. Consider that
every single day, each and every one of us is trusting in many
things that are outside of ourselves for our very existence. You
and I are trusting in things we can't see. You trust that there will
be air to breathe. You trust for your next heartbeat. You trust for
the gravity that keeps you anchored to earth.

Think about this for a moment: The earth upon which you
are standing is spinning at over 900 miles per hour, and while it
is spinning it is flying through space at over 19 miles per second.
The entire galaxy itself is racing through space at over one million
miles per day. And if the force of gravity that keeps you in place
were either increased or decreased just a fraction, then you and
everything else on the planet would go flying off into outer space.

Consider that while you are perched on this spinning orb,
each of your heartbeats is controlled by an electrical charge that
tells it to beat at just the right time. This mysterious electric
impulse that keeps your heart beating is beyond your ability
to control. What about the DNA sequencing in your body that
tells the protein chains how to align in order for your cells to
reproduce? Those DNA instructions are far too complex to have
aligned themselves by random chance.

- Who fashioned those DNA instructions?

- Who keeps the earth on its orbit?

- Who keeps the force of gravity constant?

- Who keeps your heart beating in rhythm? It is something wholly and completely outside of you. Who is it, or what is it?

Whether or not you admit it, you are indeed trusting in things you cannot see and cannot fully understand. You are trusting in something (either God or some other force) for each and every second of your life. Whether or not you acknowledge it, each day of your life, you are trusting in some force greater than yourself for your very life to be sustained. Statistically, your mere existence on this earth is miraculous

> You are either trusting in random chance, or in some higher authority who designed and sustains your existence.

and well beyond your ability to control. You are either trusting in random chance, or in some higher authority who designed and sustains your existence.

Many people refuse to confess a belief in God because they have not seen Him. I would submit that all anyone needs to do to see Him is to open one's eyes and look around. Consider the complexity of creation. It bears the imprint of its designer.

Inherent in all of us is a sense that we are dependent upon a higher power. Polls consistently show that between 96-97% of Americans believe in God or in a supreme being. Yet, so many of us find it so hard to trust Him for the things we need. Scripture commands us to trust Him for our daily needs such as the food on our table, the clothes on our backs, our employment, and our health. Yet our human nature is to doubt, to be anxious and to worry.

Each of us is trusting in something for the things we want and need, whether it is physics, random chance, ourselves or God. And one of the most important and foundational principles laid out in Proverbs is that you must trust in God in order to truly succeed in this life—to have the life that you were meant to live. Your willingness to trust God is the single biggest factor that determines the course of your existence.

We've seen this repeatedly in history. Solomon and the entire nation of Israel knew this principle well because of an event that occurred about 475 years before Solomon's reign. The moment marked a turning point in the history of the Jewish people when the nation as a whole was called upon to decide if it would

> Your willingness to trust God is the single biggest factor that determines the course of your existence.

trust in God for their existence. King Solomon was acutely aware of it, as was all of Israel. It was an historic, milestone event in the founding of the nation of Israel that left a lasting imprint upon the Jewish people. We read about it in Exodus 16, and its importance merits mentioning here.

The setting was roughly 1400 B.C., about forty-five days after Moses had led the Israelites out of slavery in Egypt. The newly freed Israelites had seen the miraculous and powerful hand of God demonstrated to them in ways that no other people had until that time, or have since. Their families had suffered hundreds of years of brutality at the hands of the Egyptians. Then God had brought Moses to them as their deliverer. God had used Moses to strip a prideful and stubborn Egypt of its wealth and of its desire to hold the Israeli slaves. Through Moses, God had turned the Nile River to blood, brought the plagues of insects, hail, darkness, disease and finally a judgment of death upon Egypt's first-born children and livestock. By the time the plagues were completed, both the Pharaoh and the people were more than willing to see the Israelite slaves go free.

The Israelites had won their freedom, and in addition, the Egyptians gave them their gold and jewelry as they left on their journey to their promised homeland. A few days after the Israelites left Egypt, Pharaoh changed his mind and sent his army out to bring them back. And you probably know what happened next. God allowed the Israelis to be trapped between the Egyptian army and the Red Sea, and God parted the Red Sea for the Israelis to pass through—a truly amazing event, like nothing ever seen before. Not only did the Israelis pass through unharmed, but when the Egyptian army passed through to pursue them, the water closed in on the charging soldiers and the Egyptian army was destroyed. So again, these Israelis saw God miraculously intervene to protect them. And just three days later, when the wandering Israelis were without fresh water, God provided the water by miraculously purifying a polluted well.

This brings us to the Exodus 16 account. Just a few days after the miraculous water purification in the desert, the Israelis had become frustrated, were desperate for food and angrily confronted Moses about their conditions. Now, if you've ever been in that area of the world, you know how dry and desolate it is and how one might feel empathy with their plight. But when one understands the context in which they are grumbling, things appear quite different. Exodus 16:2-3 describes it this way,

> And the whole congregation of the people of Israel grumbled against Moses and Aaron in the wilderness, and the people of Israel said to them, "Would that we had died by the hand of the Lord in the land of Egypt, when we sat by the meat pots and ate bread to the full, for you have brought us out into this wilderness to kill this whole assembly with hunger.

So here you have a people that within the last few months, had seen multiple miracles and had seen God bring judgment upon

Egypt. They had made the great exodus from Egypt, had the wealth of the nation given to them upon their leaving, saw the Red Sea parted, the Egyptian army destroyed, and water miraculously purified. They had seen miracle after miracle—more than any other people in history, and yet here they are complaining that *because they were hungry* then God must have brought them here to die. They tell Moses they wish they had died in Egypt.

What an insult. They had learned nothing in the months building up to that moment. They had learned nothing of God's protection and provision. Can you imagine Moses' reaction to their unbelief? He must have been beside himself with anger and frustration.

This refusal to trust God was extremely offensive. Again in Numbers 14 when the people were preparing to enter the Promised Land, ten of the spies sent out to survey the land cowered in fear of the powerful people and armies that occupied the land. They refused to believe in God's guidance and protection to take and possess the promised land of Canaan. As a result, God instructed them to turn around and prohibited them from entering their promised land. He allowed this entire generation to live the rest of their lives wandering in the desert. That entire generation of people died during the forty years of wandering in the desert. God waited for the next generation to step up to the plate, a generation that would trust him. Only a people that trusted Him could take the land and settle it.

If you or I could go back in time and speak to this stubborn people of Exodus 16 and Numbers 14 we might say something like: *Certainly your circumstances are tough right now. Yes you are hot, tired, and thirsty, but you really have no idea how much God wants to do with you. He wants to make you into the most prosperous nation on the earth. He wants to make you not just into a distinct and noble people of honor, but into THE model nation for the rest of the world. He wants to show Himself to the world through you. If you will only be still and listen, He will blow you away. You can't even begin to imagine how much God will do with you and through you if you trust Him.*

All they could see was their hunger. God wanted to use them to do things that they could not have even imagined. If they only would have humbled themselves and listened to Him and allowed themselves to be taught by Him. Just think how different their future would have been. That generation had witnessed the miraculous deliverance from slavery, and would have also seen their new nation established in their own homeland. But because of their unbelief, and their lack of trust, that would be left to their children.

The application for you and me today is profound. We often see things through the same eyes of the Israelites of Exodus 16 and Numbers 14. So many times all we see are our circumstances. Our hunger instinctively tells us that our circumstances are unfair and that we've been given a raw deal. Our doubt and fear convince us that our circumstances are beyond God's ability to deliver us.

Yet, just as in these two passages God is saying, "Look to me. I want to be your God. I want to be your provider." He has a plan for that is tailored for you. Just for you. But in order to find it and live in it, you must trust Him.

> Trust in the LORD with all your heart,
>     And do not lean on your own understanding.
> In all your ways acknowledge him,
>     and he will make straight your paths. (Prov. 3:5-6)

The trust that He is asking for is not a trust in a benign supreme power, or an impersonal force. This request describes placing your trust in the God of Abraham, Isaac and Jacob. In Yahweh. The God of the Bible. This God wants a personal relationship with you. He created you. He created you with a free will. The Fall (Adam and Eve's sin) brought all of humanity (including you and me) under the judgment intended for Satan and his legions of fallen angels. As a result, you and I were born into a fallen state and are alienated from our creator. Each and every one of us is born into sin and is under the dominion and authority of sin. We are under judgment and helpless to do much about it. Our own efforts to rescue ourselves fall short. We cannot redeem ourselves.

But God has graciously provided a means of redemption. When the chief priests and elders of Israel ordered Jesus to be crucified, He was the spotless, perfect sacrifice. He was born of a virgin and had not inherited sin and knew no sin, yet He became sin for us by taking our sin upon himself. This perfect sacrifice was the atonement for all those who have been forgiven since Jesus' death, and for all those who placed their trust in the Levitical sacrifices before his death. His atonement saves prospectively and retrospectively. And because of this, we can judicially be declared not guilty. Theologians use the term atonement or justification to describe what Jesus' sacrificial death means for us.

When Jesus died he also satisfied God's wrath. Jesus' death satisfies God's wrath against us. You see, God's justice requires Him to judge our sin. Yes, Jesus shed His blood for you and me, but more accurately His blood was shed to satisfy God's righteous requirement that a proper sacrifice be paid. The theological term for this satisfaction of God's justice is propitiation. Jesus became the propitiation for our sins.

Jesus' death also rescues us or frees us from the power of sin. His death ransoms us from the grip that sin has over us. Much like a slave must be purchased in order to be set free, Jesus' death ransoms us and frees us from the grip of sin and death. We can become born again, made alive spiritually, and adopted as God's child. The Bible teaches that after His death, Jesus defeated death and the grave's power over humanity by His resurrection from the dead, and His resurrection gives us assurance of our destiny; we can be with Him when this life is completed.

Atonement. Justification. Propitiation. Resurrection. All made possible by the death of Jesus.

Without His death, redemption would not be possible and the reassertion of His rule on earth would not be fulfilled. His mission, though His death and resurrection, was to save human-ity and to establish His kingdom rule in the earth. Jesus was not a victim. His life wasn't taken from Him. He laid it down willingly. It is the keystone event in God's plan for world redemption and kingdom rule.

The death of Jesus has profound implications for every man, woman and child. It means that if you become His follower and submit your life to His control and authority, you can start over. You can be free of sin, guilt, and shame. You can enter a per-sonal relationship with God that will continue when this life is over. You can let God change you into the person He wants you to become. You can overcome evil, and you can start this great adventure with Jesus.

This is a big decision, certainly not one to be entered into lightly. Indeed, it is the most profound and important decision you will ever make. God wants to end your alienation. Will you let Him?

If you'd like more information on how to trust Christ to rec-oncile you to God, turn to the end of this book on page 185 and read the section entitled: What does Jesus Ask of You?

**Principle: Trust God with your future.**

**Life Lesson: If you've never placed your trust in Christ to reconcile you to God, do so today.**

# 27

# BE WILLING TO RECEIVE SPIRITUAL CORRECTION

This book is about learning. It is about being teachable. It is about being humble and willing to listen. Willing to admit that we don't start off with all the answers. And so, it is fitting that this book should end on this topic.

Receiving Christ as your Savior—allowing Jesus' atoning sacrifice to redeem you from a life of sin and condemnation—is the most important decision you will ever make. To discover, accept, and apply Christ's atoning sacrifice is to find eternal life. To have the assurance of an eternity with God after this life is completed is of value beyond description. It's a value that cannot be overstated.

And yet, it is more. Following Christ is also the beginning of a new life here and now. It is a new birth. Because of Christ's atonement, the new believer comes alive spiritually. Whereas before they were estranged from God, now they are quickened to new life. When a person allows Jesus' atoning sacrifice to reconcile him or her to God, a supernatural event occurs. The theological term for this event is regeneration. The Holy Spirit of God actually comes to take up residence inside the physical body of the new believer. Jesus referred to this experience in John chapter 3 as being born again. And the apostle Paul describes a new believer in Christ as a newborn baby. And like all newborn babies, a new Christian must learn how to live this new life they've been given. And one of the key roles the Holy Spirit plays in our lives is that of teacher. Jesus desires that we grow in this new existence. In order to grow, we must be teachable like a small child. We must be humble students; we must be disciples.

When you begin a relationship with God through Jesus, His Son, you have just started becoming a learner. Finding salvation in Christ is not a destination—it is just the beginning of a long journey. Too many leaders in the Christian church have led people to pray a "sinner's prayer" only to leave these new believers as orphans without proper care and feeding. If a pastor or spiritual leader has led you to believe that praying a prayer to "receive Christ as your Savior" will cause all your problems to be over, then they have done you a disservice. Praying to receive Christ as your Savior is only the beginning of your new life. And if you aren't intentional in your spiritual growth, purposefully trying to grow in your relationship with God, then you are in for some frustrating times.

> Finding salvation in Christ is not a destination—it is just the beginning of a long journey.

I believe that one of the greatest challenges that the church faces today is a crisis of discipleship. Christian leaders of the previous generation and of my generation have failed to disciple the next generation of believers responsibly. Part of that failure is the failure to communicate the expectation to new believers that they must become disciples.

A disciple is one who learns and, when needed, accepts correction. Scripture says that God corrects those He loves. If we are willing to be corrected, God can shape us and He can use us. If we refuse to be corrected, if we rebel against the Holy Spirit that is now living inside of us, and seeks to change our attitudes and our character, then we diminish, suppress and frustrate the Holy Sprit's efforts to help us grow spiritually.

Chapter 2 of this book focused on being teachable. Just as a willingness to listen and become teachable is paramount for students to learn in the natural world, spiritual correction is indispensable to spiritual growth. If a believer in Christ says that he or she is attempting to "grow spiritually," i.e., willing to cooperate with the Holy Spirit as He seeks to mold us into the image of Christ, yet is in practice unwilling to receive spiritual correction, that person will remain immature and childlike—and like any other person who refuses to listen to others, will exhibit many of the qualities of a "fool."

> If a believer in Christ says that he or she is attempting to "grow spiritually,"... yet is in practice unwilling to receive spiritual correction, that person will remain immature and childlike—and like any other person who refuses to listen to others, will exhibit many of the qualities of a "fool."

Unfortunately this happens all the time. There are many, many people that make a sincere decision to follow Jesus, and yet refuse to continue in the posture of a disciple by being unwilling to be corrected by either God's Holy Spirit or by other people. You may know people like this. I know people that live like this. You may see yourself or someone close to you in this description. Such a person is an immature Christian, a believer who has refused (or by his passivity has neglected) to become a disciple.

In Chapter 9, we faced a very sobering question: What if this "fool" that Proverbs so often repeatedly describes is someone close, such as a family member? What if the fool that Proverbs is describing is a spouse? This is quite a challenge. It happens all the time. While it is true that all of us will occasionally act in foolish ways, some people, because of their continued refusal to be teachable, are in a very difficult place that makes it equally difficult for those around them. They can develop character traits that are extremely unattractive.

Regarding marriage specifically, Scripture is abundantly clear that the marriage covenant is sacred and the admonition in Proverbs 14:7 to leave the presence of a fool does not give a spouse license to end a marriage. Let there be no confusion on that point. If a close family member has the character traits described in Chapter 9, then a lack of willingness to listen and to be corrected is likely at its root. Some form of loving correction is needed, such as marriage counseling, personal counseling, mentoring or a combination thereof.

If you find yourself in this situation, understand that there is hope for you because of the life-transforming power of God. Remember that we are all in a dynamic (changing and not static) relationship with God, and as such we are all in the process of growing. Even though your loved one may not be maturing as quickly as you would hope, remember that God is committed to their progress. God is in the people-changing business. That's what He does. This transformation process is called *sanctification*. It means that a person is becoming transformed into the personality and character traits of Jesus Himself and Scripture says that God is committed to sanctifying those who call on His name. He is constantly moving to help us (your loved ones included) change to become more

> God is in the people-changing business. That's what He does.

patient, more loving and more giving. So, despite what you see in the natural realm, it is possible for people to change their ways.

This kind of change is what God has committed Himself to. Understand that it is a process that takes time. It happens when people recognize their need for change and when they engage in the types of consistent lifestyle adjustments needed to make it happen. Your part in this process is to pray for God to show your loved one their need to change. And that is a prayer that He will answer.

And at the same time, your part is to be committed to also change in the way that God directs. God is just as committed to changing you as He is committed to changing your spouse. Often a stubborn or wayward spouse is most impacted by seeing their spouse demonstrate the Christ-like qualities that God is committed to building in every believer.

All around you are examples of people whose lives have been radically transformed by God because they listened to the people who were able and willing to speak into their lives the life changing truths they needed to hear. By cooperating with God's Holy Spirit, they have grown into more loving, caring, selfless people. In many cases, they have been delivered from addiction and rescued from abuse or paths of self-destruction. They are people that our society and even many of their friends had given up on—people who looked like they were beyond hope—people like Victoria Childress. Growing up in a broken home, she began cutting herself as a means of coping with the lack of love and affirmation from absent parents. Through God's love, Victoria overcame her self-destructive habits to find both physical and emotional healing. You can see her story at http://www.iamsecond.com/seconds/victoria-childress/.

Another example is Duche Bradley of Dallas, Texas, who overcame a life of anger, violence and crime to find forgiveness and freedom from self-destructive behavior. Two common factors that Victoria and Duche have in common are that they each have embraced a willingness to be corrected. And, they have those around them that didn't give up on them. They have those around them that they can ask:

- "Am I teachable?"

- "What adjustments can I make in my life to become a better spouse, a better wife, husband or father/mother?"

- "What misconceptions or attitudes do I need to adjust in order to become more sensitive to the needs of others?"

- "Where are my blind spots?"

- "What can I learn from this situation?"

This is humility. And this is the starting point in your relationship with God. This is the appropriate place to begin, for it allows God to mold us. It allows God to change us.

**Principle: Be willing to receive spiritual correction.**

**Life Lesson: Ask those close to you if you are teachable.**

# 28

# CONCLUSION

In the Introduction, I stated that life is not fair. This is true. Life is not fair because you and I see circumstances through fallen eyes. We have a flawed standard of "fairness." One's circumstances and position in life, wealth or standard of living, physical beauty, talent, or physical ailments may be the end-all standard that we so often use to judge whether we have received our "fair share" in this life. But our limited and flawed assessments and standards are not the standards that God uses to measure the quality of our life or the value of our life. Rather, these external circumstances are actually tests of our character. Scripture is very clear that those who are given more are held to a higher standard of accountability in their stewardship responsibilities. We are stewards of what we have. This is the responsibility of everyone, regardless of whether you have little or have much. To whom little is given, little is required. And to whom much is given, much is required. If you have been blessed with much, you are accountable for much. This is sobering.

We've seen that Proverbs describes that "doing wisdom," or acting wisely, is like a sport to a wise man. If you want to be wise, then make it like a sport. Exercise wisdom for the sake of doing it—for its intrinsic value. Decide to act wisely for wisdom's sake.

Just as Tiger Woods or Steve Largent practiced to become the best in their fields, practice being wise. Become wise for the sake of being wise.

> Exercise wisdom for the sake of doing it—for its intrinsic value.

Start with the small things, like looking people in the eye when you talk to them. Like taking notice of the tone in your voice when you talk to your children. Treat people with dignity and respect. People notice these things more than you know. These are the kinds of behaviors that earn favor with people. They will respond accordingly. Their tone of voice will change. You will begin to have more influence, which in turn builds your confidence.

Start with the everyday things that are closest to you, the things over which you have the most control. Start with the small, immediate decisions that you overlook and take for granted every day. Start with things such as:

- How you talk to your spouse.

- How you spend your money.

- How much money you are saving.

- How you spend your time.

- What you eat.

- The words you say.

- The words you don't say.

- How much you exercise.

Begin to put into practice what you have read in the last twenty-seven chapters.

When faced with a decision, ask yourself, "What is the wise thing to do?" Start small, with the mundane, everyday situations: Should I make that comment, or hold my words? Should I spend that money or save it?

As you begin to put wisdom into practice, begin to take an inventory of your life. Ask yourself:

- What am I doing to seek wisdom?

- Am I putting myself in tempting situations?

- Am I surrounding myself with foolish people?

- Am I hanging out with wise people, people who encourage me? People who have something to offer? Or am I hanging out with people who gossip, criticize others and are a negative influence on me?

- Am I eating poorly?

- Am I wasting my time?

- Am I sowing destructive seeds into relationships around me by speaking harshly to others?

- Am I a gossip?

- How can I be wise in this situation?

- Who can help mentor me in this area?

- Who can point out my blind spots?

- Who can help here?

- What is God trying to show me here?

- Am I cooperating with God's attempts to change me here, or am I rebelling against what I know He is asking of me?

Ask people you trust to help identify areas where you can apply wisdom. They will tell you.

If you start applying wisdom consistently to the small decisions you make, you will become wise in many things. As you start your inventory, make a list of the behaviors you will change and adjust your behavior accordingly. Do it for a trial period of time and see what happens. People will see you differently and treat you differently. If you will do these things, people will notice. If you're married, believe me, your spouse will notice.

Practice it. Then purpose to make it a way of life.

Remember, doing wisdom is like a sport. Do it for the sake of doing it. Learn to receive pleasure from doing wise things, and Proverbs 2:5-11 will come alive for you.

> Then you will understand the fear of the LORD
>     and find the knowledge of God.
> For the LORD gives wisdom;
>     from his mouth come knowledge and understanding;
>     he stores up sound wisdom for the upright;
>     he is a shield to those who walk in integrity,
>     guarding the paths of justice
>     and watching over the way of his saints.
> Then you will understand righteousness and justice
>     and equity, every good path;
>     for wisdom will come into your heart,
> and knowledge will be pleasant to your soul; discretion will
>     watch over you, understanding will guard you.
>     (Prov. 2:5-11)

May you walk in wisdom.

# PRINCIPLES AND LIFE LESSONS

### The Nature of Wisdom

Wisdom is available to everyone: You can choose to be wise.

You must be teachable: Humble yourself and be willing to learn.

You must listen: Learn to listen and practice becoming a good listener.

You must seek wisdom: Seeking wisdom means learning to apply it and practice, practice, practice.

### The Power of Words

Words are the most powerful tool in your life: Recognize the power of words, and choose your words carefully.

Guard your words: Don't talk too much.

Gossip destroys people: Don't gossip.

### Relationships, Family & Sex

Guard your affections: Be careful to whom you give your heart.

Stay away from fools: Be selective with whom you spend your time, and in whom you place your trust.

Don't commit adultery: Take the necessary steps to protect your marriage and your sexual purity.

Discipline your children: Make the discipline of your children a priority.

Learn to control your temper: If you have a bad temper, make it an immediate priority to seek help to adopt the skills needed to manage your anger.

Respect the opinions of others: Learn to guard your reaction to other peoples' opinions.

Live in Community: Purposefully place yourself in close relationships with others.

## Personal Management, Business & Finance

Live on a budget: Develop a personal household budget and stick to it.

Persistent, hard work will pay off: Work diligently and save diligently.

Laziness will result in poverty and debt: Learn to embrace work, labor and inconvenience so they can equip you for success.

Dishonest business practices do not bring lasting success: Apply honesty and integrity to your business.

Your reputation is more valuable than your possessions. Protect your reputation by living consistently.

There is no shortcut to wealth: Establish a financial strategy based on reasonable expectations, not through presumption or schemes that require no time, effort or money, or that rely on chance.

Don't contractually obligate yourself on behalf of others: Only co-sign a loan if you can afford to (and are fully prepared to) be the one that pays it off.

Keep money in perspective: Don't make the acquisition of money or possessions the goal of your life.

Generous people will be benefit from their generosity: Become a generous giver. You will benefit from it.

## Spirituality

The fear of the Lord is the beginning of wisdom: Bow your knee in humble acknowledgement that God is sovereign over you.

God is in control: Understand that God is moving in and through events to accomplish His purposes.

Trust God with your future: If you've never placed your trust in Christ to reconcile you to God, do so today.

Be willing to receive spiritual correction: Ask those close to you if you are teachable.

# LIFE LESSONS

**The Nature of Wisdom**
Choose to be wise.
Humble yourself and be willing to learn.
Learn to listen and practice becoming a good listener.
Seeking wisdom means learning to apply it and practice,
practice, practice.

**The Power of Words**
Recognize the power of words, and choose your words
carefully.
Don't talk too much.
Don't gossip.

**Relationships, Family & Sex**
Be careful to what and to whom you give your heart.
Be selective with whom you spend your time, and in whom
you place your trust.
Take the necessary steps to protect your marriage and your
sexual purity.
Make the discipline of your children a priority.
Make it a priority to adopt the skills needed to manage
your anger.
Learn to guard your reaction to other peoples' opinions.
Purposefully place yourself in close relationships with others.

**Personal Management, Business & Finance**
Develop a personal household budget and stick to it.
Work diligently and save diligently.

Learn to embrace work, labor and inconvenience so they can equip you for success.

Operate your business with honesty and integrity.

Protect your reputation by living consistently.

Establish a financial strategy based on reasonable expectations, not presumption or schemes that require no time, effort or money, or that rely on chance.

Only co-sign a loan if you're willing to (and are fully prepared to) be the one that pays it off.

Don't make the acquisition of money or possessions the goal of your life.

Become a generous giver. You will benefit from it.

## Spirituality

Bow your knee in humble acknowledgement that God is sovereign over you.

Understand that God is moving in and through events to accomplish His purposes.

Place your trust in Christ to reconcile you to God.

Ask those close to you if you are teachable.

# WHAT DOES JESUS ASK OF YOU?

The claims of Jesus are unique from all other leaders of history, and from all other religions and belief systems. He is the incarnation; the God of the universe that stepped into human history to reconcile us to Him. This is who Jesus claims to be.

If you have come to believe this also, then you are faced with a critical question: What does Jesus ask of you?

Many people believe in Jesus. But it is not enough to just "believe in" Him or to give mental assent to the facts surrounding the events of His life, death and resurrection. It is not enough to simply believe that He lived or to even recognize what He has done for humanity and for you personally. No, Jesus calls each of us, you and me, to be His follower. He wants to be your Lord, your boss.

This is a big ask. And many are not willing to accept it.

Jesus faced a man like this once. You can read about this man in Matthew 19. He said, *Jesus I know from what I've seen you do, the miracles etc., that you are the answer that I'm seeking, so what do I need to do?* And Jesus told him to follow Him above all other priorities. The man went away sad because he just couldn't bring himself to do that. There were too many other competing priorities in this man's life of which he wasn't willing to let go. And Jesus didn't chase after him and try to negotiate. Jesus didn't offer to cut him a deal. Jesus knew the man wasn't ready to completely surrender his own agenda and become a follower, a learner, a disciple. And so Jesus let the man go away. Perhaps the man eventually became a follower of Jesus. Perhaps he didn't. We don't know. But Jesus didn't attempt to minimize the requirement.

Becoming a follower of Jesus is not easy.

Following Jesus means yielding to His will for your life. It means He becomes the boss. Jesus said,

"Not everyone who says to me, 'Lord, Lord,' will enter the kingdom of heaven, but the one who does the will of my Father who is in heaven." (Matt 7:21)

Too many church leaders have inadequately presented Jesus' "offer" of salvation. They use terms like "ask Jesus to come into your life" or "ask Jesus into your heart." This is a woefully inadequate communication of what is being required of those who seek to follow Jesus. Consider these two statements of Jesus,

"Whoever loves father or mother more than me is not worthy of me, and whoever loves son or daughter more than me is not worthy of me." (Matt. 10:37)

"Then Jesus told his disciples, 'If anyone would come after me, let him deny himself and take up his cross and follow me.'" (Matt. 16:24)

This is radical. This is not an invitation to join a club, or add some new item or element to your lifestyle. This is an invitation to come and die. Put to death your own desires, and your own nature, and through that to find life itself. A new life. An authentic life. A life that is reconciled to your creator.

## It Requires Important Decisions

If you become a follower of Jesus, God will not be your co-pilot. He owns the airline. And He owns the airspace in which the plane flies. And becoming His follower requires that you recognize this and organize your life and priorities accordingly. It requires some important decisions.

First, Jesus requires that you repent of your rebellion against God. He requires that you turn from your sinful nature and accept His offer of reconciliation to God. In doing so, you must commit to follow Him and yield to His will for your life.

He must become the guide and director of your life, your attitudes and your priorities. When you make that decision, you allow your will to come into alignment with His will. Your entire worldview starts to adjust according to His priorities. The apostle Paul referred to this process as a transformation. He instructs that followers of Jesus should become "transformed by the renewing of your minds" so that you can see God's will played out in your life.

And if you are willing to do this, then you get to experience all the benefits that this relationship with God brings.

Following Jesus (or choosing not to follow Jesus) is the most important decision a person will ever make. Not just because it will determine one's eternal destiny, but also because it defines (or re-defines) one's identity now. Yes, Jesus' offer to follow Him is free to receive, but it will actually cost you everything, in that you have to be willing to lay aside every other priority in your life that would supplant your allegiance to Him.

## *What Does This Look Like on a Practical Level?*

Following Jesus doesn't mean that you join a church, that you follow a person or group into strange religious doctrines, or that you check your brain at the door. It doesn't require joining a religious cult. But it does require that you be willing to turn from whatever He calls you away from— sinful actions, unforgiveness that you may be harboring toward someone, or whatever is not aligned with His will for you.

But whatever you have to leave behind, He will replace with other things that are tailor made for what you need. He knows what you need better than you do. And His plans for you are good.

If you want to follow Jesus, you can start right now. You can start by praying a prayer of commitment to Jesus. Something like:

> *Dear Jesus, I confess my rebellion against you and against God the Father, my creator. I renounce my reliance upon myself. I can't do life on my own anymore, and I don't want to. I want you to save me, to change me, to adopt me and to bless me. Holy Spirit come and invade my life, every part of me. Rule me today, dear God. Today I turn from my sinful ways and commit to follow you in all I do. I know I will make mistakes but from this day forward I trust you to show me how I should live. So take my life and make it all that you want it to be.*

If you have sincerely prayed this prayer and meant it, then:

- You are now clean. Judicially declared "not guilty."

- You are now forgiven.

- Your sin and offenses against God have now already been judged (Jesus took the punishment for you).

- You stand righteous before God as if you've never sinned.

- The Holy Spirit has adopted you.

- You are now a new creature in Christ.

This is truly amazing! Truly astounding, isn't it? What's next? If you have made this decision, you need to tell someone. Call a friend, someone you trust. Tell them about what you did. This decision to follow Jesus is not merely a private affair. You are a new creature. You have a new nature. You are now re-born spiritually. Congratulations! Your new adventure begins.

The Bible gives several analogies for someone that has found new life in Jesus. Your new life is like a new seedling plant, or like an infant child that needs acute nourishment and care. So next, you need to get involved with other believers in Jesus in a local church congregation where you can form meaningful relationships with other believers.

Above all, begin reading the Bible. Jesus describes the Bible as the "Word of God." And He likens it to food. He also likens it to water. He said that we literally can't live without it; we will starve if we don't get it. So read it. Memorize it. Devour it. Drink deep. Let it teach you. Let it change you.

If you have prayed this prayer, then please drop me an email to let me know at *decision@onlinelifelessons.com*. This link was created just for this purpose. Email addresses received by this link will not be sent any special offers. We will not ask you for money. We won't give this list to anyone. And we won't sell it. In fact, we won't even attempt to communicate with you through it, other than an automatic response you'll get to let you know that we have received it. We just want to know if the time and effort we have put into this book is reaching people.

Life with Jesus is an adventure. It is the ultimate adventure. As you begin your journey, I wish you every success!

# ENDNOTES

1    See "How Rich was King Solomon?," The Bible Study Site, last visited September 13, 2017, http://www.biblestudy.org/basicart/how-rich-was-solomon.html; Happy Riches, "What is the estimate of king Solomon's wealth in today's economy and is he the likely richest?," last visited September 9, 2016, http://www.quora.com, What-is-the-estimate-of-king-solomons-wealth-in-todays-economy-and-is-he-the-likely-richest, and the following business site give about 100 billion, Abe Oluwasegun, "King Solomon Wealth: How Much Was Solomon Worth?," (January 25, 2015, last visited September 13, 2017, http://www.practicalbusinessideas.com/king-solomon-wealth-net-worth). He certainly would have rivaled the richest people in the world today in net worth.

2    Lydia Saad, "Three in Four in U.S. Still See the Bible as Word of God," Gallup.com (June 4, 2014, last visited September 13, 2017, http://www.gallup.com/poll/170834/three-four-bible-word-god.aspx).

3    For Larkin's story, see http://www.iamsecond.com/seconds/nate-larkin/ (last visited February 2, 2018)

4    For Nickels's story, see http://abiliworksinc.blogspot.com/2009/11/alone-in-arctic-story-of-alaskan.html (last visited February 2, 2018)

5    Swati Arora, "Robert Friedland mentor to Steve Jobs," Famous mentors and their famous mentees (October 15, 2002, last visited September 13, 2017, http://www.mentorpolis.com/famous-mentors-and-their-famous-mentees/).

6    Andrew Clarkson, "The Ice Warnings Received By Titanic," July 25, 2017, http://titanic-titanic.com/warnings.shtml.

7    Eric Page, New York Times, "Mel Fisher, 76, a Treasure Hunter Who Got Rich Undersea," (December 21, 1998, http://www.nytimes.com/1998/12/21/us/mel-fisher-76-a-treasure-hunter-who-got-rich-undersea.html); Ronnie DeGhetto, Mel Fisher, The Greatest Treasure Hunter of All Time" (August 23, 2016, https://www.thegolddigger.com/blog/news/mel-fisher-greatest-treasure-hunter-time/); Mel Fisher, Wikipedia.org (May 23, 2017, http://www.wikipedia.org/wiki/Mel_Fisher).

8   "A word is not a crystal, transparent and unchanged, it is the skin of a living thought and may vary greatly in color and content according to the circumstances and the time in which it is used." *Towne vs. Eisner*, 245 U.S. 418, 425 (7 January 1918).

9   Christiane Northrup, M.D., Mother-Daughter Wisdom: Creating a Legacy of Physical and Emotional Health (Bantam, 2005).

10  Associated Press, "Jackson's death returns his father to the spotlight," June 29, 2009, MSNBC, http://www.msnbc.msn.com/id/31633663/; last visited August, 2009; and "Janet Jackson on Facing Her Demons, Fighting Her Fears, and Healing a Lifetime of Hurt," *EBONY*, December 1997).

11  I heard this story from Craig McConnell when he was speaking at a conference in Colorado, 2011.

12  Ken Blanchard and Barbara Glanz, *The Simple Truths of Service (Book Only): Inspired by Johnny the Bagger* (Simple Truths, 1ˢᵗ ed., July 1, 2005).

13  BrainyQuote, "Abraham Lincoln Quotes," https://www.brainyquote.com/quotes/authors/a/abraham_lincoln.html, and BrainyQuote, "Mark Twain Quotes," http://www.brainyquote.com/quotes/authors/m/mark_twain.html; http://thinkexist.com/quotation/it_is_better_to_keep_your_mouth_closed_and_let/215886.html.

14  Samuel Greengard, "Gossip Poisons Business—HR Can Stop It," *Workforce* (July 2001, last visited September 13, 2017, http://www.workforce.com/2001/07/15/gossip-poisons-business-hr-can-stop-it).

15  Barbara Hatcher, "Winston Churchill's Integrity," *Vital Speeches* (March 1, 1987, last visited September 13, 2017, http://www.bible.org/illustration/winston-churchill's-integrity).

16  Jen Schefft, *Better Single Than Sorry: A No-Regrets Guide to Loving Yourself and Never Settling* (Harper Collins, 2007), p. 39.

17  John Holt, *How Children Learn* (Cambridge, MA: Da Capo Press, rev. ed, 1967), 56.

18  Tom W. Smith, "American Sexual Behavior: Trends," Socio-Demographic Differences, and Risk Behavior, National Opinion Research Center at the University of Chicago, GSS Topical Report No. 25 Updated March, 2006.

19  Janice Abrahms Spring, *After the Affair: Healing the Pain and Rebuilding Trust When a Partner Has Been Unfaithful* (New York: William Morrow; 2ⁿᵈ ed.), p. 9.

20  Emily M. Brown, *Affairs; A Guide to Working Through the Repercussions of Infidelity* (Hoboken, NJ: Jossey-Bass, Sept 1999), 171.

21   CPT Charles L. Bryner, Jr., M.D., "Children of Divorce: Consequences of Divorce," *J. Am Board Fam Med* 2001;14(3), (quoting from web article, last visited September 13, 2017, http://www.medscape.com/viewarticle/405852).

22   Judith S. Wallerstein, & Sandra Blakeslee, *Second Chances: Men, Women and Children a Decade after Divorce* (New York: Ticknor & Fields, 1989), 298-99.

23   Catherine Valenti, The Devastating Economics of Divorce, ABC News web article April 16, 2017 (she quotes Natalie Nelson) The Devastating Economics of Divorce - ABC News – last visited September 13, 2017, http://abcnews.go.com/Business/story?id=87208&page=1 via @ABC.

24   Janis Abrahms Spring, *After the Affair: Healing the Pain and Rebuilding Trust When a Partner Has Been Unfaithful* (New York: Harper Collins, 2012), p. 46-47.

25   Jane Johnson Struck, "Surviving the Affair by Connie Neal as told to Jane Johnson Struck," *Christianity Today* online, March 1999 (http: http://www.todayschristianwoman.com/articles/1999/march/9w2096.html, last visited January 30, 2018.

26   Jane Johnson Struck, "Surviving the Affair by Connie Neal as told to Jane Johnson Struck," *Christianity Today* online, March 1999, (http://www.todayschristianwoman.com/articles/1999/march/9w2096.html, last visited January 30, 2018.

27   Tara Parker-Pope, "T. Berry Brazelton on Self-Esteem, Discipline and Learning From your Kids," (http://well.blogs.nytimes.com/2008/09/14/dr-brazelton-on-self-esteem-discipline-and-learning-from-your-kids, Sept. 14, 2008). "A child who has not been disciplined to learn self-control by the time he is old enough to be unsupervised by parents, or old enough to fight back at parents who spank, is a child in danger."

28   Robert Lewis, "Winning at Work and Home," Video Series, Session 10: Maximum Parenting, 2014, last visited September 13, 2017, www.mensfraternity.com.

29   Alec Baldwin, last visited September 13, 2017, http://www.imdb.com/name/nm0000285/; and Sarah Hall, "Alec Baldwin Apologizes for Phone Fury," Enews, April 20, 2007, last visited September 13, 2017, http://www.eonline.com/news/54951/alec-baldwin-apologizes-for-phone-fury; and TMZ staff, "Alec Baldwin Gives His View," April 27, 2007, last visited September 13, 2017, http://www.tmz.com/2007/04/27/alec-baldwin-gives-his-view/).

30   John Eldredge, *Waking The Dead: The Glory of a Heart Fully Alive* (Nashville: Thomas Nelson, Nov 2006), pp. 199, 200.

31   The survey of 1,003 Americans was conducted by Princeton Survey Research Associates International on behalf of the National Foundation for Credit Counseling, or NFCC, a nonprofit association of community counseling services. Reported by MSN, last visited September 13, 2017. http://articles.moneycentral.msn.com/SavingandDebt/Advice/SurveyManyAmericansIgnoreTheirFinances.aspx.

32   James A. Danoff-Burg, "The Determiners of Climate: Sunlight, Moisture, Temperature, and Wind," Module 9: Light and Temperature, last visited September 13, 2017, (http://ccnmtl.columbia.edu/projects/seeu/bio2/restrict/modules/module09_content.html).

33   A Changed Life: Brian Head Welch, Changed Lives (last visited September 13, 2017, http://www.changedlives.info/Celebs.shtml#S11); see video of his testimony, last visited September 13, 2017, http://www.iamsecond.com/seconds/brian-welch/.

34   Art Buckwald, Quotes, (last visited September 14, 2017, www.goodreads.com/quotes/178740-the-best-things-in-life-aren-t-things).

35   Christianity (Matt 7:12) Buddhism (Udana-Varga 5:18) Hinduism (Mahabharata 5:1517) Islam (Number 13 of Imam "Al-Nawawi's Forty Hadiths) and Confuciansim (Mencius VII A 4).

36   Rob Moll, "Scrooge Lives," *Christianity Today* 52 (Dec 2008).

37   Mark Blumberg, Seymour Schulich and Philanthropy Quotes, November 26, 2007, last visited September 14, 2017, www.globalphilanthropy.ca/blog/seymour_schulich_and_philanthropy_quotes.

# BIBLIOGRAPHY

"Alec Baldwin Gives His View" 2007 Retrieved from
    http://www.tmz.com/2007/04/27/alec-baldwin-gives-his-view/

Arora, Swati. (2002, October 15) Robert Friedland Mentor to
    Steve Jobs. Retrieved from http://www.mentorpolis.com/
    famous-mentors-and-their-famous-mentees.

"Art Buchwald >Quotes>Quotable Quote" (2008, Nov. 12)
    Retrieved from https://www.goodreads.com/
    quotes/178740-the-best-things-in-life-aren-t-things

Baldwin, Alec. (2007) Retrieved from http://www.imdb.com/name/nm0000285/;

Biblestudy.org (n.d.) Retrieved from http://www.biblestudy.org/basicart/how-
    rich-was-solomon.html

Blanchard, Ken and Glanz, Barbara. *The Simple Truths of Service. Inspired by
    Johnny the Bagger.* Naperville, IL: Simple Truths, 2005.

Blumberg, Mark. (2007, Nov 26) Seymour Schulich and Philanthropy
    Quotes. Retrieved from www.globalphilanthropy.ca/blog/
    seymour_schulich_and_philanthropy_quotes

BrainyQuote. (n.d.) Retrieved from https://www.brainyquote.com/quotes/
    authors/a/abraham_lincoln.html

BrainyQuote, (n.d.) Retrieved from http://thinkexist.com/quotation/it_is_bet-
    ter_to_keep_your_mouth_closed_and_let/215886.html.

Brown, Emily M. Affairs; *A Guide to Working Through the Repercussions of
    Infidelity.* Hoboken, NJ: Jossey-Bass, 1999.

Bryner Jr. M.D., CPT Charles L. (2001) *Children of Divorce: Consequences of
    Divorce.* Retrieved from http://www.medscape.com/viewarticle/405852).

Chao Chao, William. (2016, Sept. 9) What is the estimate of King Solomon's
    Wealth in Today's Economy and is He Likely the Richest? Retrieved from
    https://www.quora.com/What-is-the-estimate-of-king-solomons-wealth-in-
    todays-economy-and-is-he-the-likely-richest)

Childress, Victoria (n.d.) Retrived from http://www.iamsecond.com/seconds/victoria-childress/

Christianity (Matt 7:12) Buddhism (Udana-Varga 5:18) Hinduism (Mahabharata 5:1517) Islam (Number 13 of Imam "Al-Nawawi's Forty Hadiths) and Confuciansim (Mencius VII A 4).

Clarkson, Andrew. (2017, July 15) The Ice Warnings Received by Titanic. Retrieved from http://titanic-titanic.com/warnings.shtml.

Danoff-Burg, James A. (2000) The Determiners of Climate: Sunlight, Moisture, Temperature, and Wind, Module 9: Light and Temperature. Retrieved from http://ccnmtl.columbia.edu/projects/seeu/bio2/restrict/modules/module09_content.html.

DeGhetto, Ronnie (2016, August 23) Mel Fisher, The Greatest Treasure Hunter of All Time Retrieved from https://www.thegolddigger.com/blog/news/mel-fisher-greatest-treasure-hunter-time/)

Eldredge, John. *Waking the Dead: The Glory of a Heart Fully Alive.* Nashville: Thomas Nelson, Nov 2006. Print.

Greengard, Samuel. (2001, July) Gossip Poisons Business—HR Can Stop It. Retrieved from http://www.workforce.com/2001/07/15/gossip-poisons-business-hr-can-stop-it).

Hall, Sarah. (2007, April 20) Alec Baldwin Apologizes for Phone Fury. Retrieved from http://www.eonline.com/news/54951/alec-baldwin-apologizes-for-phone-fury;

Hatcher, Barbara. (1987, March 1) Winston Churchill's Integrity. Retrieved from http://www.bible.org/illustration/winston-churchill's-integrity).

Holt, John. *How Children Learn.* New York: Da Capo Press, 1967.

Jackson's death returns his father to the spotlight. (2009, June 29) *Associated Press.* Retrieved from http://www.msnbc.msn.com/id/31633663

Kiyosaki, Robert. *Rich Dad Poor Dad: What the Rich Teach their Kids about Money that the Poor and the Middle Class Do Not.* Scottsdale, AZ: Plata Publishing, 2011.

Lewis, Robert (2014) Maximum Parenting Video Series Session 10: Winning at Work and Home. Retrieved from www.mensfraternity.com.

Lichtman, Louis J. *A Practical Guide for Raising a Self-Directed and Caring Child: An Alternative to the Tiger Mother Parenting Style.* Bloomington, IN: iUniverse, Inc. 2011.

Mercy11 (2017, May 23) Mel Fisher. Retrieved from http://www.wikipedia.org/wiki/Mel_Fisher).

Moll, Rob. "Scrooge Lives," *Christianity Today* December 2008.

MSN (2007, April 19) Retrieved from http://articles.moneycentral.msn.com/
SavingandDebt/Advice/SurveyManyAmericansIgnoreTheirFinances.aspx

Northrup, Christiane M.D. *Mother-Daughter Wisdom: Creating a Legacy of Physical
and Emotional Health.* New York: Bantam, 2005.

Oluwasegun, Abe. (2017, Decembeer 30) King Solomon: How Much Was Solomon
Worth? Retrieved from http://www.practicalbusinessideas.com/2015/01/
king-solomon-wealth-how-much-was-solomon-net-worth.html).

Page, Eric (1998, December 21) Mel Fisher, 76, a Treasure Hunter Who Got
Rich Undersea. Retrieved from http://www.nytimes.com/1998/12/21/us/
mel-fisher-76-a-treasure-hunter-who-got-rich-undersea.html)

Parker-Pope, Tara (2008, Sept. 14) T. Berry Brazelton on Self-
Esteem, Discipline and Learning From your Kids. Retrieved
from http://well.blogs.nytimes.com/2008/09/14/
dr-brazelton-on-self-esteem-discipline-and-learning-from-your-kids.

Randolph, Laura. "Janet Jackson on Facing Her Demons, Fighting Her Fears,
and Healing a Lifetime of Hurt," *EBONY*, December 1997.

Saad, Lydia. (2014, June 4) Three in Four in U.S. Still See the Bible as Word of
God. Retrieved from http://www.gallup.com/poll/170834/three-four-bible-
word-god.aspx).

Schefft, Jen. *Better Single Than Sorry: A No-Regrets Guide to Loving Yourself and
Never Settling.* New York: Harper Collins, 2007.

Smith, Tom W. (2006) "American Sexual Behavior: Trends. Socio-Demographic
Differences, and Risk Behavior," National Opinion Research Center at the
University of Chicago, GSS Topical Report No. 25 Updated March, 2006.

Spring, Janice Abrahms. *After the Affair: Healing the Pain and Rebuilding Trust
When a Partner Has Been Unfaithful.* New York: Harper Collins 1996.

Struck, Jane Johnson. (1999, March) Surviving the Affair. Retrieved from
http://www.todayschristianwoman.com/articles/1999/march/9w2096.html

*Towne vs. Eisner.* 245 U.S. 418, 425 Supreme Court of the United States 1918.

Valenti, Catherine. (2017, April 16) The Devastating Economics of Divorce.
Retrieved from http://abcnews.go.com/Business/story?id=87208&page=1
via @ABC.

Wallerstein, Judith S. and Blakeslee, Sandra. *Second Chances: Men, Women and
Children a Decade after Divorce.* New York: Ticknor & Fields. 1989.

Welch, Brian. (2017) A Changed Life: Brian Head Welch, Changed Lives
Retrieved from http://www.iamsecond.com/seconds/brian-welch/.

# ABOUT THE AUTHOR

Terry Allen is a consultant to some of the largest and most successful companies in America. For over 30 years he has worked in all phases of public policy development. A veteran strategist with expertise on a broad range of issues, from technology policy and tax policy, to health care and nutrition policy, he also serves as a leading political consultant for candidates at all levels.

Allen is also committed to the *Great Commission*. He is the founder of www.onlinelifelessons.com an innovative web platform that licenses feature films to promote evangelism and discipleship. He works in Washington, D.C. He and his wife Laurie have 5 children and 2 grand-children.

Made in the USA
Columbia, SC
13 August 2024

40442361R00115